The Shape of Actions

The Shape of Actions
What Humans and Machines Can Do

Harry Collins and Martin Kusch

The MIT Press
Cambridge, Massachusetts
London, England

This book was set in Sabon by Wellington Graphics and was printed and bound in the United States of America.

Library of Congress Cataloging-in-Publication Data

Collins, H. M. (Harry M.), 1943–
  The shape of actions : what humans and machines can do / Harry Collins and Martin Kusch.
    p. cm.
  Includes bibliographical references and index.
  ISBN 0-262-03257-0 (hc. : alk. paper)
  1. Human-machine systems. 2. Automation. I. Kusch, Martin.
II. Title.
TA167.C65   1999
620.8′2—dc21   98-36125
                                                        CIP

To
Charlie Chaplin
and
Nick Faldo

Contents

Preface

At the University of Oulu in Finland in 1991 the authors fell into argument over dinner. That interchange developed into a full-blown partnership in a project that resulted in this book. Most of the theory is a joint product of the two authors working things out in front of a blackboard during intense discussions occurring in large part in Bath and Edinburgh. Neither author could have written the main sections of the book on his own.

We are particularly grateful to Gerard de Vries and Wiebe Bijker for allowing us to use in chapter 5 some of the ideas *taken from H. M. Collins, G. de Vries, and W. Bijker, "Ways of Going On: Skill, Action, and Behavioural Repertoires," Science, Technology and Human Values,* 22, 3 (1997), 267–284. That chapter also draws on Collins's "The Structure of Knowledge," *Social Research,* 60 (Spring 1993), 95–116, while chapter 7 draws on his "Rat Tale: Sociology's Contribution to the Problem of Human and Machine Cognition in Context," in P. J. Feltovich, K. M. Ford, and R. R. Hoffman, eds., *Human and Machine Expertise in Context* (Cambridge, Mass.: AAAI/MIT Press, 1997), 293–311. Parts of the conclusion rest on Collins's "Embedded or Embodied: Hubert Dreyfus's *What Computers Still Can't Do," Artificial Intelligence,* 80, 1 (1996), 99–117.

It is not unusual for a book to include previously published work, but in this case it is not a matter of our collecting existing papers; rather it is the other way round—the book project gave rise to the papers. Given the project's interdisciplinary nature, and its attempt to treat the topic in a way that is quite out of step with almost every other approach, including those of the authors' parent disciplines, we thought it appropriate that some of the principal ideas should be tested by the peer review process of leading journals before inclusion in the book. That is why we are particularly pleased to be able to report the above sources and to note that two of the other chapters have passed scrutiny in a form very similar to that in which they appear here. Chapter 3 has been tested in the philosophical marketplace, and the bulk of it has appeared as H. M. Collins and M. Kusch, "Two Kinds of Actions: A Phenomenological Study," *Philosophy and Phenomenological Research, 55,* 4 (1995), 799–819. Chapter 9 has been examined and extensively improved through its exposure to historians of technology and is an almost unaltered version of H. M. Collins and M. Kusch, "Automating Airpumps: An Empirical and Conceptual Analysis," *Technology and Culture, 36,* 4 (1995), 802–829.

We are grateful to the editors of all the above-mentioned sources for permission to reproduce either the ideas or the words that they originally saw fit to allow to be published. In every case we have gained immensely from the advice and criticism of referees and editors.

We must also thank the many colleagues and students who forced us to think through and develop what we were saying. The students at the University of California at San Diego, to whom Collins taught some of these ideas in the spring of 1993, were generous in their understanding and sharp but constructive criticism. We have already thanked our Dutch colleagues, de Vries and Bijker, and should not pass by without mentioning some other friends at the University of Limburg and their students— notably Annemiek Nelis, who forced us to work out various bits of the theory during her brief time as an exchange student at Bath. Colleagues at Bath who were generous with their time include Graham Cox and David Gooding, while the Bath Science Studies Centre students did much to keep the project going; they include Georgina Rooke, Warren Evans, and Robert Evans. Tom Gieryn of the University of Indiana commented on the book at the American Sociological Association meeting in Washington, D.C., in August 1995 in an especially constructive and useful way, helping us to see more clearly our theory's relationship to Max Weber's notion of behavior. Jon Clark, of the University of Southampton, gave generously of his time in reading and commenting on the manuscript. In addition, Kusch in particular wishes to thank Bernie Katz

(Toronto) for discussions about Donald Davidson; Bryan Boddy, Dennis Klimchuk, and Niko Scharer for joining him in a philosophy of action reading group in Toronto in the spring of 1992; and Riitta Korhonen (Helsinki), Heini-Eliisa Hakosalo (Oulu), Simon Schaffer (Cambridge), David Bloor, John Holmwood, Matthias Klaes, Donald MacKenzie, Stanley Raffel, and Carole Tansley (all Edinburgh) for objections, suggestions, and examples. We have also benefited from the feedback at the many conferences and seminars that offered the opportunity to rehearse our themes. Naturally, all remaining mistakes and infelicities are our responsibility.

All in all, our critics have commented with varying degrees of sympathy, but they have always done it forcefully; it seems that whatever we are doing, we are not just following the trend. We accept this, and we hope that we have done a good enough job explaining our position in this book that the trend will turn.

The collaboration that led to this book was made possible in part by ESRC grant R000234581.

Cardiff University
Cambridge University
July 1998

1

Humans and Machines

What can humans do? What can machines do? How do humans delegate actions to machines? How do humans cooperate, and what kind of social organizations are there? How do humans exploit other human cultures?

These questions can be answered with a new theory: the theory of the shape of actions, or action morphicity. The theory goes like this: Humans can do two kinds of actions and—like machines—they can merely behave. When humans do *polimorphic actions,* they draw on their understanding of their society; when they do *mimeomorphic actions,* they intentionally act like machines—entities that do not need to understand society; when humans unintentionally blink or jerk their knees, they are like machines in every respect except appearance and moral worth.[1] Machines cannot do polimorphic actions because they do not have an understanding of society on which they can draw; but, though machines do not have intentions, they can be made to mimic mimeomorphic actions. It is obvious that if humans can act in ways that mimic machines, then, to that extent, machines can mimic human actions.

Why do we talk about the "shape" of actions—or action "morphicity"? It is because the theory of morphicity, unlike any other theory of action we know, is concerned with what actions look like from the point of view of an observer. From the outside, two mimeomorphic actions will,

1. The basic distinction between two kinds of action was put forward in Collins (1990) using a different terminology. In this book the terms "polimorphic action" and "mimeomorphic action" replace Collins's earlier usage "regular action" and "behavior-specific action" (or "machinelike action"). The old terminology was not sufficiently "intuitive"; the terms did not carry enough information and the verbal formulations did not contrast clearly enough to be memorized and easily applied.

in principle, look the same; and we say that they have the same shape. Polimorphic actions usually look different on repeated occurrences. We also use diagrams to show the relationship between the "shapes" of different types of actions and to elaborate our theory.

There are entities that can do polimorphic actions and entities that cannot. We call all entities that cannot do polimorphic actions "machines." This gives the term a broad extension. The machines we discuss include bridges, fridges, boots, bikes, bureaucracies, rockets, canoes, car washes, computers, machine tools, paint sprayers, plaster casts, animals, armies, air pumps, and McDonalds. We do not discuss insects, trees, rocks, and rivers, but we might have done so and, if we had, we would have called them machines as well.

We also use "machine" in its more conventional sense to refer to the elements of the above list that typically include gears or silicon chips. There is nothing confusing about this; in our theory, the relations that hold between humans and machines-as-conventionally-understood are the same as those that hold between humans and machines-as-defined-under-our-broad-extension.

For the sake of brevity, we call all entities that can do polimorphic actions "humans." It is not clear whether nonhumans, such as chimpanzees and dolphins, can do polimorphic actions. If it turned out that dolphins and chimpanzees could do polimorphic actions, we would call them humans rather than machines. But the question does not arise in this text. Babies and, perhaps, autistic persons cannot do polimorphic actions, but we refer to them as humans because of their biological and moral continuity with other humans.

The key dichotomy between polimorphic and mimeomorphic actions is superficially similar to other dichotomies discussed in philosophy and the human sciences, but it divides the world in a different place, and it divides actions in a different way. The differences will become apparent in the text and will be discussed in the conclusion.

Boundaries

What has counted as the boundary between humans and machines, humans and animals, and science and nonscience, has varied from time to time and place to place. Challenging, exploring, and demonstrating the permeability of these boundaries (a task to which the current authors have each made a small contribution) have given rise to some of the most exciting, not to say liberating, changes in our understanding of how the world is constituted. From one perspective, our current project continues this work: We show that the boundary between humans and machines is permeable at least insofar as humans often find reason for acting in machinelike fashion. We explore the possibility of shifts in the position of the boundary between humans and machines: If humans changed the ways they acted, they could make the very boundary between themselves and machines disappear.

But the essence of the theory of the shape of actions is to establish new boundaries rather than analyze or question old ones. We believe we have discovered a principled difference between those entities in the world that can do polimorphic actions and those that cannot. We could not understand how the boundary between humans and machines might shift if we had not first discovered the difference between polimorphic and mimeomorphic actions.[2] We are realists where our new dichotomies are concerned, and this allows us to be relativists about other things. We are realists when it comes to human beings and their actions, and thus we can be relativists about the way these actions make the world. Humans could have a world in which the boundary between machines and themselves became invisible, but to do this they would everywhere have to change the way they act. Were this to happen, the difference between polimorphic and mimeomorphic actions would remain; it is just that the terms would apply to different sets of actions in the world.

Plan of the Book

Our emphasis moves from theory to application. The early chapters are a theoretical defense and elaboration of the major dichotomy of actions, illustrated with examples drawn from common experience. The later chapters show the way the divisions can be applied, using more substan-

---

2. We use the word "discover" quite self-consciously to mark our commitment to social realism. For a more complete discussion, see Collins and Yearley (1992).

tive examples. In the first part a taxonomy of actions serves to brace the major dichotomy against attack from borderline cases; apparently fuzzy cases are shown to fall into subclasses on one side of the dichotomy or the other. The taxonomy also provides terms that are important in applications of the theory.

The new theory we develop, as we will show in the conclusion, splits the world in a different place to every preceding and superficially similar theory. Most of these preceding theories have a long and distinguished history and are very well established, yet we are going to argue that they miss the really important point. To realize such a grand ambition and defend it against all imaginable criticisms and counterexamples is not a trivial matter; inevitably, then, the first few chapters are densely argued. Those who would like to see where the whole thing is going before they commit themselves could jump ahead to chapters 6, 7, or 8, and have a look at the conclusion. (Chapter 9 is, again, rather specialized.)

In chapter 2 we explain what we mean by a theory of action, and we set out the methodological assumptions and presumptions that underlie the approach, which is a combination of sociology and philosophy.[3] The difference between polimorphic and mimeomorphic actions sheds an interesting light on the idea of a social science and on the different varieties of order that are found in society.

Chapter 3 divides polimorphic action into three types and mimeomorphic action into four types, giving examples of each and accounting for apparent counterexamples to the main dichotomy and for fuzzy cases.

Using the seven types of action, chapter 4 works out the significance of the theory of the shape (morphicity) of actions for interactions between

---

3. Kusch has used the term "sociophilosophy" to describe such an approach. He is engaged in a reconstruction of philosophical epistemology based on "epistemological collectivism"—the view that the primary subject of knowledge is the group, not the individual (Kusch 1996, 1997, 1998).

"Philosophical sociology" is another description of what we do here—the study of formative action types, or the way types of human action make up societies. The two projects are two sides of the same coin. We see it as following the tradition of the later Wittgenstein (1953) and of Winch (1958). Both of these authors see conceptual structures as the counterpart of patterns of activity within forms of life or, as we might say, social collectivities. Given this way of looking at things, investigating the way that people do things is to investigate the way they think about the world, and vice versa.

people and people, and between people and machines. To make sense of what people do, one must share their society or form of life. Therefore machines ought to be the strangest of strangers. The most difficult problem our theory must deal with is not the gaucheness of some machines but the savoir faire of others.

Chapter 5 refers to the seven types of action to reveal what is involved in humans' learning new skills and actions. Some standard cases, such as bicycle riding, are shown to have been incorrectly analyzed in the past.

Chapter 6 employs the theory and its categories to analyze the action of writing. We move from high-level actions, such as writing a love letter, to low-level actions, such as inscribing individual symbols of the alphabet on the page.

Chapter 7 begins with a study of machines for writing and moves on to develop a typology of machines based on what machines do, and to another interwoven typology turning on how machines work. The difference between types of machines can be seen only by using the subcategories of the theory.

Chapter 8 applies the major dichotomy to organizations. We argue that the process of bureaucratization and deskilling has typically been cast at too high a level; this is why it has repeatedly failed to anticipate the problem of replacing humans with machines. The notion of mimeomorphic action is crucial to understanding such organizations as restaurants and armies.

Chapter 9 is an application of the major dichotomy to the technological development of the air pump. We show that the shape of actions provides the key to understanding the processes of mechanization and automation.

In the conclusion we pull together what we see as the consequences, both big and small, of what we have proposed.

2
Methods and Principles

What Is a Theory of Action?

Actions can be divided into two broad types, which relate differently to the behavior that instantiates them. The terms "action" and "behavior" are already the property of many different academic discourses and, since there already exists a huge literature on the philosophy of action, we need to clear some ground.[1]

To understand what we mean by actions, one must first understand what we mean by society and what we mean by "form of life." Societies differ: In British society in the 1990s we can go to the cinema, drive to work, play darts, supervise a student, take out a mortgage, and so on. If we were members of the Azande society studied by Evans-Pritchard, we could do none of these. We could, however, accuse someone of being a witch, prepare *benge*, consult the poison oracle, and invoke spirits; in current British society we can do none of these. The reason we could do some things in one society and not in another has little to do with what is legal and illegal, and everything to do with the differing social and conceptual structure of life in the two societies. It does not make sense to do the things in one society that do make sense in the other.[2] We are going to refer to those things one can intentionally do in a society, that get their sense from taking place in that society, as "actions."

1. Anscombe (1979), Chisholm (1970), Danto (1973), Davidson (1982), and Goldman (1970).
2. Note that having read Evans-Pritchard's (1937) accounts of the Zande, we could "go through the motions" of doing some of these things in our own society, but we would not really be doing them.

Going to the cinema is an action; preparing benge is an action, and so forth.

We do other things that are not actions. Blinking is not an action. "Accidentally knocking over the table as a result of running through the house" is what philosophers would refer to as an action, but it is not the type of action that interests us. In the case of knocking over the table, our usage is different from the regular usage in the philosophical literature. In the case of blinking, our usage seems to be in accord with standard philosophical usage. A blink is something that happens to us, it is not brought about by something we do. A blink is merely a piece of *behavior.* But we will also use the word "behavior" in an extended sense; behavior includes all physical movements and therefore includes the physical movements humans use to execute the actions they intend.

Actions, Intentional Actions, and Formative Actions

Action Types and Tokens
The kind of actions that interest us are a subset of the kinds of actions that traditionally interest philosophers. We will be studying and classifying *types of intentional actions.*[3] This emphasis upon types rather than *tokens* of intentional actions sets our project apart from the academic tradition, which deals with responsibility for actions and the logical form of action sentences. We are, then, studying and classifying action *types* like "(intentionally) greeting," "(intentionally) swinging a golf club," or "(intentionally) singing a song." We are not studying action *tokens*, like Mary greeting John at 7:32 A.M. on Friday the 29th of October 1993, or like Fred singing "As Time Goes By" at 12:15 P.M. on the 5th of January 1992, except insofar as they usefully represent and illustrate action *types*.

Intentional Actions: Their Results and Their Consequences
Because of the stress upon types of *intentional* actions, we are able to avoid problems that have to do with the unintended consequences of intentional actions or with unsuccessfully executed intentions to act. Thus we are not concerned with actions such as "launching a torpedo

3. Our notion of action is similar to that of Carlos Moya's (1990) "meaningful actions" (see chapter 4); see also Rubinstein (1977).

as a result of accidentally pressing the torpedo-launch button while intending to ring for the steward." Nor are we concerned with the action of "missing the target" (except as it illuminates the meaning of trying to hit the target), and so forth. While for some analysts of action, the unsuccessful execution of intentions to act are themselves instances of types of actions (i.e., after all, "failing to open the door" can have many different instances), they are not, ceteris paribus, types of *intentional* actions. (Unless of course one fails intentionally.)

Generally speaking, the *result* of an action is the state of affairs that has to obtain for that action to have been carried out, whereas the *consequence* of an action is a further state of affairs that has been brought about by the attempt to carry out the action. The *result* of an action is conceptually linked to the intention while the consequences are contingently related only.[4] If John opens a door and lets in cold air, we would say that the result of the action was the door being open, and the consequence was cold air entering the room—*unless* John intended to make the room cold by opening the door, in which case the cold air entering was also a result.

An example drawn from fiction shows nicely the difference between the results and consequences of actions. In John Le Carré's (1963) novel of the Cold War, *The Spy Who Came in from the Cold,* Smiley, the controller of Leamas, a British spy, gives him the job of saving one East German spymaster and destroying another. The sensitive and refined Fiedler has been accused of being a traitor by the vicious Nazi, Mundt; Leamas is to save Fiedler and destroy Mundt. Leamas is told to assume the identity of a malcontent defector from the British Secret Service.

The ruse succeeds and Leamas is picked up by the East Germans and asked to give evidence at a secret trial. Leamas "betrays" the Nazi, telling the court that it is Mundt, not Fiedler, who has been working for the British. Mundt's defense is that Leamas is a British plant, but the court does not believe Mundt. At this point Leamas believes he has achieved the intended *result* of his actions. He believes he has saved Fiedler, who has been helping the British, at the expense of Mundt, by concocting the tale of Mundt's treason and having it believed by the East Germans.

4. See von Wright (1971).

Then Leamas's cover is blown and it becomes clear to the court that Mundt was right in accusing him of being planted by the British. Leamas's actions will not have the result he wanted; in fact they will have a *consequence* that is the opposite of what he intended. Fiedler is condemned and Mundt reinstated.

Later we learn that this was always Smiley's plan. Mundt, Nazi that he is, *is* a traitor to the East Germans and *is* working for the British; Fiedler is not. Smiley arranged for Leamas's cover to be blown at the crucial moment in order to save the vile Mundt at the expense of the honest Fiedler, who is in fact loyal to his own country, not to Britain.

Let us summarize: Leamas's intention was to save Fiedler at the expense of Mundt; that was the desired *result* of his actions. The unintended *consequence* of what he did in pursuit of that intention was to save Mundt at the expense of Fiedler. Note that for some philosophies of action, but not for ours, one would say that Leamas's action was to save Mundt. In our language, to save Mundt at the expense of Fiedler was Smiley's action and his alone; this was the intended *result* of Smiley's actions. Smiley used Leamas's quite different intention as a means of carrying out his own actions.[5] The unintended *consequences* of Leamas's intention to act were the intended *result* of Smiley's actions.

Formative Actions
In one way the stories of Leamas and Smiley are poor examples of actions, as we use the term. To make the point, we will have to introduce a neologism. We differ from the majority of writers in the philosophy of action in that we are concerned with types of actions that constitute a community, a collectivity, or a form of life. Such actions make a society what it is and distinguish it from other societies.[6] We call such actions

---

5. We will later develop the notion of an "action cascade." In an action cascade, one person's actions are included in the actions of another. Here Leamas's actions are included in the action cascade set in motion by Smiley.

6. The authors uncovered the differences in the extension of the term *action* that seem "natural" to philosophers and sociologists respectively only after many days of frustrating discussion. To a sociologist it seems perverse to use the same word "action" to refer not only to things we do intentionally that relate to the way we live, but also to accidents and unforeseeable consequences. A term with that

"formative actions."[7] Members of the same form of life share in a common net of concepts and actions. That is to say, they agree in their concepts because they share a realm of possible actions, and they agree in their actions because they share a common network of concepts. Actions and concepts are tightly intertwined because intentions are conceptual, and because concepts provide guidance for actions. This internal-essential link between concepts and actions notwithstanding, within a form of life some types of intentional actions are more formative (or constitutive) than others. Think, for example, of the form of life of Catholics in general, and the ritual during a mass in particular. It is not central to the ritual of a Catholic mass whether the priest sings along with the congregation. If, however, he was not to perform the action of praying for the transubstantiation, or if he did not lead the congregation in saying the Lord's Prayer, most Catholics would feel either that the mass had not been performed *properly*, or had not been performed at all. We suggest calling these latter two actions, praying for transubstantiation and saying the Lord's Prayer, *formative* of the Catholic form of life (or at least, of the form of life of the mass).

The borderline between formative and nonformative actions is fuzzy, and historically and culturally variable. After all, it is easy to imagine a sect within the Catholic Church that regards the *singing* rather than the *saying* of the Lord's Prayer as absolutely essential for the successful performance of the mass ritual. That the borderline between formative

---

extension seems to the sociologist about as useful in the context of social science as a term that covers, say, all bicycles and all blue things. We discovered, eventually, that the sociologists' "actions" corresponds to what many philosophers would call "types of intentional actions."

7. We would have preferred to use the term "constitutive," but this term is usually contrasted with "summary" or "strategic" as in constitutive and summary rules or constitutive and strategic rules. In our terminology, summary rules are as much constitutive of a form of life as are constitutive rules. Compare the rules of soccer as played by the Brazilian national team—a matter of graceful short passes—and by Wimbledon Football Club—a matter of getting the ball into the opponent's penalty area as soon and as often as possible by long kicks upfield. In these cases only the summary rules are different, the constitutive rules being common to both styles of play. Nevertheless, the two forms of soccer life are different and are associated with a different range of possibilities of formative actions on the part of the players.

and nonformative actions can change does not mean, however, we are unable to draw a distinction in day-to-day practice. In fact, in many instances we are easily able to list a fair amount of formative action types belonging to different forms of life. Think for instance of the formative action types for different sports, for various games, for parliamentary sessions, for shopping, negotiating, lecturing in front of an academic audience, and so forth, and think of particular things that one might do in such settings that are not formative. Sometimes, of course, one innovates in such settings in the hope of changing a form of life and instituting new ways of going on.

Much of the philosophy of action has been developed in terms of examples that are not formative in our sense. Philosophers have concerned themselves mainly with examples of individual cases of assassinations, accidental killings, doing "this" while intending to do "that," and so forth. This follows their preoccupation with questions of responsibility and causality, but the one-sided diet of examples has had the unfortunate effect of removing the whole issue of the interrelations between actions and forms of life from philosophers' sight. From now on, unless otherwise indicated, we will use the term "actions" to mean "types of intentional actions that are formative."

Actions, Institutions, and Fractals

Formative action types are social institutions, and they constitute social institutions. Let us sketch what we mean by an institution.[8]

What makes a metal disc "a coin," or a piece of paper a token of value, that is, what makes such things instances of money? It is, of course, that a collective treats the items as money, that it talks of them as money, that it uses them as money, and that it sanctions and enforces this talk and this use. If the collective ceases to believe that the paper and coins are money, and that they have the value represented symbolically on their surfaces, these items cease to be money. This is not just a philosophical nicety but a practical problem, as inflationary spirals, and the precautions that governments take to prevent them, reveal.

8. For the performative model of social institutions, see also Anscombe (1974), Barnes (1983), Bloor (1997), Kusch (1997, 1998), Lagerspetz (1995), Searle (1995), and Tuomela (1995).

The institution of money is such that money ceases to exist if those who take part in the institution cease to act as though it exists. Both analysts and actors agree on that feature of money. In another kind of case, such as that concerning the notion of "mountain," there is no question that the institution includes the idea that mountains would continue to exist even if the actors ceased to act as though they existed. We will use this distinction between "social kinds" and "natural kinds" in the analysis that follows.[9] There has been much argument about the ways in which the two types of institution, those referring to social kinds and those referring to natural kinds, differ. For example, is the continued existence of mountains in the absence of actors' beliefs about them to be treated as a feature only of the social institution of mountain or a feature of mountains themselves? But this argument is of no importance in this book.

Different societies have different social institutions; even when they have the "same" institution, they realize this "same" institution in different ways. For example, in the case of money, the guarantee might be reserves in gold, or the authority of a chief. Let us call this conventionality.

The mutual belief that sustains institutions is self-referring; the referent of the belief is the belief itself. On analysis, actors' belief that a certain token is money turns out to be the belief that other actors also believe the same tokens to be money. The value of the money is nothing but mutual belief in the value of the money (or belief in the guarantee that lies behind it). It is also self-validating; it is the mutual beliefs that make the beliefs true.

Given the way such institutions are formed by mutually reinforcing beliefs, and given that this mutual reinforcement must be continual, it is not surprising that the form of social institutions is not fixed nor predetermined by any formula.[10] Obviously institutions must be bounded

9. See also Barnes (1983), Bloor (1996, 1997), and Kusch (1997, 1998).

10. Barnes and Bloor refer to this feature of social institutions as "finitism." The term contrasts with philosophical accounts in which the meaning of a term is taken to be its extension over an infinite set of instances. In Barnes and Bloor's treatment, as in ours, meaning is based on a finite body of experience (Barnes, Bloor, and Henry 1996; Bloor 1997).

and rule following in some sense, or they would not be recognizable as institutions, but the way they are lived out is continually up for renegotiation—at least at the boundaries. Moving from context to context, actors continually reconstitute the institution through their decisions and actions. Such judgments are unavoidable, but they are underdetermined by past instances.

That judgments of how to act in new instances cannot be arbitrary is ensured by the fact that they must be collectively justifiable within the institution. In this sense, the "rule following" is not congruence with a formula, but mutual recognition that no mistake has been made.

The need for collective acceptance in social institutions makes the actions of members predictable; as we would say, it is one way in which action coordination is ensured. In this sense, formative action types are social institutions.

If we take forms of life to be larger sets of formative actions, they too can be understood to be institutions as described above. Thus there is a similarity of structure from "small" formative actions all the way up to whole forms of life. Think, for example, of the form of life of *sport* compared to the form of life of *war*. Each is driven by different ideas of what is appropriate to do. What counts as making a mistake is different in each. In sport it is not proper to kill to win, whereas it is proper in war. In sport (at least in some countries), it is considered better if the sides are reasonably fairly matched, whereas responsible leaders in a war will try to gain overwhelming superiority before committing their troops to battle. If a side of twelve-year-olds beats a side of five-year-olds by two hundred runs to two runs in a game of cricket, it will be said to have been a game organized by a fool, but when the ratio of casualties in the Gulf War was of the order of 10,000 to one, the allied generals were considered to have had matters well organized. The nature of these two social institutions—sport and war—is constituted and maintained by self-referential mutual beliefs.

Moving down to smaller examples, one finds, within the form of life of sport, the forms of life of individual sports. As social institutions these have again the same self-referential and self-validating "logic." Sports differ not only in their encoded rules, but also in what is generally accepted as proper ways of going on. Thus in golf (so we are told), it is expected that any infringement of the rules will be reported even if it was accidental, and even if the infringement was witnessed by no one but the golfer him- or herself. For example, if a player, unseen by anyone else, and gaining no advantage from it whatsoever, accidentally touches the sand in a bunker before hitting the ball, he or she is expected to report the misdemeanor and penalize him- or herself by the appropriate number of strokes. In modern professional soccer the opposite way of going on seems an integral part of the game: Soccer players will do all they can to hide their own infringements while pretending that others have fouled them, in order to have their opponents penalized unfairly.[11] It does not seem unreasonable to say that forms of life are embedded within one another as separate sports are embedded within sport as a whole.

It is not only forms of life that differ; roles within forms of life differ according to the types of acts that can sensibly be done within them. And again, self-referential mutual beliefs fix the nature of these roles. When we are supervising students we can suggest some reading, suggest a line of analysis, demand a piece of written work by a certain date, criticize

---

11. Golf is full of bizarre examples of players penalizing themselves. *The Observer* newspaper of Sunday, 7 November 1993, reports on page 5 of the sports section that the golfer Martin Poxon disqualified himself from a competition, and from automatic entry to all European tour events for the following season, by reporting a mistake that had no other conceivable consequences. During a competition played in very wet circumstances his ball ended up in a puddle on the putting green. Following what he thought was the correct procedure, he picked it up and dropped it away from the puddle but no nearer the hole; the resulting position happened to be off the green and on the "fairway." The ground being very wet, the rule in force that day was that a ball might be lifted from the fairway and placed in a "preferred lie" no nearer the hole and within six inches of its initial position. Poxon proceeded to "lift and place." The rule he had unwittingly broken, and that he did not discover he had broken until some time later, was that the ball should not have been dropped in the first place but should have been placed directly on the spot from which it was to be played. When compared to the antics of soccer players, the self-reporting of this mistake, with its devastating consequences, could not better express a difference between two forms of life. (We need not mention the bizarre consequences that befall a sport that tries to anticipate every eventuality in its rule book rather than relying on the good sense of officials and players. Golf is a good example of a misplaced attempt to eliminate polimorphic actions.)

the use of the passive voice, and so forth. We can't do any of this when we are, say, giving a public lecture at the university, though lecturing is just as much a part of our academic form of life as is supervising students.

Going still further down the scale, what we can do within roles also differs. When we are criticizing the use of the passive voice in a piece of written work, we might explain that it is often found in "scientific" literature to imply the lack of agency of the author. We might explain that it tends to take vitality out of the writing, we might point to particular sentences and show how they might be rewritten, and we might suggest the use of a style-checking software. Note, once more, that the Azande can do none of this, nor can we do it when we are giving a public lecture, nor can we do it when we are "demanding a piece of work from a graduate student by a certain date," even though the latter is still part of graduate supervision. Supervising a student is an action, criticizing use of the passive voice is an action, and suggesting the use of style-checking software is an action, though each of these actions is embedded within the previous one. And, again, what makes these actions the actions they are is that a group collectively takes these actions to be what they are, that is, the group constitutes them as these actions.

There is a mathematical idea that illustrates how, from actions all the way up to forms of life, we always can reidentify the same structure: the structure of self-reference, self-validation, conventionality, and lack of predetermination of what it is to follow a rule. This is the notion of the fractal. A fractal is a mathematical structure that retains its form no matter what the scale. The coast of Norway is a standard example: seen on the map, the coast of Norway has jagged inlets called fjords; each fjord, however, has its own jagged inlets so that the coast of a fjord has roughly the same form as the whole coast of Norway but on a smaller scale; each inlet within a fjord, if examined more closely, again has the some form, and so on down the scale.

The structure of forms of life and the actions that are embedded within them is like a fractal; their philosophical/sociological "morphology"—the self-referential, and self-validating structure of mutual belief—is preserved as the scale is reduced. Occurrences of fractal-like entities in nature do not have the purity of the mathematical structure; the similarity of form does not go on forever. In the case of Norway, by the time you get down to grains of sand, the sequence is broken. The same is true of the form of life/action fractal. If we go a few steps further down the scale of what we do when we supervise a student, we can no longer be said to be acting. Thus in criticizing the use of the passive voice, we will be expelling air from our lungs—no longer an intentional action.

The fractal idea seems to capture the connection between the embedding social entity and the embedded social entity: In both, ways of thinking about things and ways of doing things are intimately connected. Thus there is a link between forms of life writ large (societies), forms of life within societies (war, sport), and forms of life writ smaller still (individual sports). As we go on down in scale we find ourselves no longer talking of forms of life, but of actions typically executed within them, and these again are linked in a fractal-like sequence. To understand actions as we use the term, it is important to see that the meaning of actions and forms of life are related all the way up and all the way down.[12]

A Technical Language for Actions

"When we do activity X, we do a lot of polimorphic actions and only a few mimeomorphic actions." "Activity Y was once typically performed with polimorphic actions, but in modern times it is more usually done with mimeomorphic actions." "In this group the activity consists largely of polimorphic actions, but in that group the same activity is constituted largely of mimeomorphic actions." One problem in making this kind of claim sound convincing is that the normal labels that cut up our activities are taken from everyday talk, and the way everyday talk divides action does not fit tidily with our new technical categories. Suppose we say, as we will say, "swinging a golf club is a mimeomorphic action." Someone

12. Collins and Pinch (1982) discussed these issues in connection with their studies of parapsychology. They felt that parapsychology and orthodox science were best understood as separate paradigms, or forms of life. Thus within one of these forms of life the results of an experiment would be seen as signifying one thing, whereas in the other form of life, the same experimental result might be seen as signifying its opposite. There were, however, high-level elements in common, such as the notion of experiment itself.

might remark to us that they swung a golf club only yesterday and did it after the fashion of a polimorphic action. That we open ourselves to this kind of response is a result of our trying to express ourselves briefly. What we should have said is: "Since the 1930s when someone swings a golf club, and that person is trying to swing the golf club according to the method recommended in the contemporary coaching manuals that help to make up the form of life of modern golf, then they are doing a mimeomorphic action." Actually, that is how most people do try to swing golf clubs today, and we allow ourselves the luxury of abbreviating the exact long formulation by the shorter "swinging a golf club is . . . , etc." The usage is sociological; it expresses something about how things are generally done in this society and how they are expected to be done.

We claim that if we explained what we meant about different types of action to actors in any particular sphere of action, they would be able to see what we were getting at within their practice, even though the concepts we bring to bear are "technical concepts." Technical concepts are ways of describing the world that are not in widespread use. Even if the occasions on which the two types of golf swing were practiced in real life were horribly intermingled, a golf player would still be able to see that there are two types. Nevertheless, seeing what is going on in terms of types of action can sometimes be hard because we have such a fixed idea of how we do things that we are often unable to reflect properly upon them.

Individuals, Society, and "Internal States"

We have said that we are concerned not with particular actions done by particular individuals on particular occasions, but with action types that are formative of societies. This does not mean we can escape entirely from what goes on in peoples' heads. Actions, as we use the term, are tied up with intentions, and intentions are internal states. It is impossible to be sure about internal states. When it is important to identify individual internal states, as in assignment of responsibility for crimes, huge and costly institutions are set up to investigate them. Despite these purpose-built institutions, intentions are sometimes misidentified. But attributing an internal state to an individual is quite different from investigating the internal states that are plausible features of a form of life. That we can never be sure whether we have uncovered the motives of a murderer is not the same as saying that we can never be sure whether or not basely motivated murders take place in our society. It is easy for us to understand how this *type* of action could take place, even if we cannot be sure that we have correctly identified any one of its instances, or tokens. We can understand that basely motivated murders could take place because we are participants in the society and because we know that murder is a feature of it.

Suppose that every night between twelve and one we engage in certain movements that we think of as doing a rain dance, with the intention of making it rain the following day. Sometimes we believe we are successful, and sometimes not. The idea of a rain dance has to be familiar to us if we are to think of ourselves as rain dancing, but at the same time we are sure that the performance of dances meant to bring rain is not part of any of the forms of life pertaining to British society. What sort of "sureness" is this? It is the sureness of the enculturated participant in the society. Getting to know the kinds of actions that might reasonably and regularly be done in a society is a lot easier than identifying whether some action was actually done by an individual. It is this kind of sureness that allows sociologists to discuss, say, the differences between Zande and Western society.[13]

Though getting to know individual motives is the province of priests, psychiatrists, and judges and juries rather than of sociologists or anthropologists, some part of coming to participate in a society involves talking to individuals. Asking individuals to discuss their intentions is one of the ways in which we might develop our understanding of how aspects of society work in general. In these cases the concern with individuals is the way they represent general patterns of action. Individuals are indices of the nature of the underlying collectivities.

Intention and Consciousness
What we have said so far might be misconstrued as meaning that an intentional action is always something that follows on a consciously

13. It would be a problem not only for interpretative sociology but even for quantitative research; even questionnaire design turns on shared understandings of what can be done in the way of asking and answering questions.

formulated intention. But an action can be an intentional action without the actor having to be aware of the intention from moment to moment. Imagine you are driving your car to work and you are changing gears while thinking about something else entirely. Then, for a moment, your attention strays back to the car driving during a sequence of gear changes. We do not want to say that the first set of gear changes were not actions while the second set were. It cannot be that what counts as an action switches around in this way depending on exactly what the actor is thinking about; that would be an unsatisfactory notion of action.

Sometimes the intentional nature of actions can be made apparent if actors are disturbed and asked what they are doing.[14] If, during your car-driving reverie, an irritating sociologist were to ask you what you were doing and why, you would be able to reply; this is one way of providing a warrant for saying the action was intentional. Nevertheless, were we to disturb a car driver who denied all knowledge of changing gears, we would still not doubt that the gear changing was an action.

As we will argue later, we do not require that actors are aware of what they are doing when they are woken from their reveries; we require only that *some* actors know what they are doing when woken from reveries; this is enough to establish the existence of a *type* of action.

What Is "The Same" Behavior?

Our theory rests upon the relationship between action and behavior, and therefore we have to discuss action and behavior as distinct from one another. One of the sorts of things we will want to say is that there are certain kinds of actions that are distinguished by our desire to perform them with the same behavior on every occasion. But to say things like this presupposes we know what we mean the "the same." We have to recognize that "the same," even when it is a matter of physical movements, is not the same for everyone. We will return to the "sociology of the same" in a later chapter. To introduce an example that we will return to later, one golf swing may feel the same as another golf swing to a golfer, especially if both result in the ball traveling the same 250 yards on the same flight path, but these two golf swings would look different

---

14. See von Wright (1971) and Dennett (1991).

to the owner of the hidden dog that is hit by the second ball landing one yard from where the first landed. An engineer watching the two swings on videotape or making measurements with a micrometer would also see them as different.

Who might be included among those whose groupings of sameness must be taken into account as we develop our theory? There is the actor, there are observers of the action who do know what action is being essayed, and there are observers who are not in a position to know what action is being essayed, or who, like the dog owner or engineer, have different interests than those of the actor. There is a tension in sports commentaries, both professional and amateur, caused by the differences in perspective. When a golfer hits a shot of, say, 200 yards that finishes within a foot of the hole, commentators and playing partners will call it a "great shot." However, a shot of this sort is no better in terms of human accomplishment than a "good shot" that finishes six feet from the hole; at that range the difference between one foot and six feet is chance alone.

Actors and knowledgeable observers might refer to groups of *physical movements* as "the same" by grouping them according to the sameness of the intentional action. Thus there is a class of soccer strikes on goal that could be taken as exhibiting the same behavior irrespective of the final position of the ball, inside or outside the net.

Let us switch examples and consider the action of uttering a certain word—for example, "you." Utterers and knowledgeable observers could agree that all mouth movements associated with saying "you" were "the same movements"—the movements required to say "you." But someone who did not understand the word "you" would be most unlikely to think that all the mouth movements associated with the myriad ways of pronouncing "you" among different people should be classed as the same; they would have no reason to see them as the same.

The class of actions we call mimeomorphic actions is the class where the kind of trouble discussed in the last paragraph need *not* occur. It is worth spelling this out:

Mimeomorphic actions are actions where exact reproduction of the *behavior* by someone who *did not understand the action* would always appear to reproduce the *action* to someone who *did understand the action.*[15]

One way this kind of act can be facilitated is by the actors always *trying* to reproduce the behavior that instantiates the act in as near as possible the same physical way each time it is essayed. Then imitators need learn to reproduce only a set of physical movements to mimic the action. Success is not guaranteed, but it is a good start.

The notion of sameness is tied to the notion of digitization—that is, making sure that there is an area of tolerance around each entity that is to count as the same.[16] It is the tolerance that makes it possible for mimeomorphic actions to be imitated by an observer because the mimicry can be inexact. Life can be made easier for uncultured imitators by making the movements "coarse grained" on the human scale. It is easier to detect arm movements than mouth movements, and if arm movements are themselves arranged into a course-grained system of categories, it is still easier. That is how semaphor works. First, words are digitized by the use of an alphabet, then, the letters are represented by course-grained arm movements.

Using semaphor, we can signal the word "you" without having any idea that we are doing it. To make "you" using semaphor we *could* simply intend the bodily movements without thinking about the word. What is more, an observer who did not speak English could mimic the movements of the arms and thus pass on the letters intended to someone who could speak English, and who would then understand the word. The coarse-grained digital system of semaphor consists of "left arm" or "right arm," with eight positions for each arm (up, down, straight out left, straight out right, and the four in-between points). In semaphor, "you" looks like:

```
\_   _\   \/
 |    |    |
 Y    O    U
```

Prior to recognizing a semaphor signal, one must recognize the categories of arm movement; how one learns to see this is a problem, but

15. And this is how the "Chinese Room" (e.g., Searle 1980) is supposed to work!
16. See Haugeland (1985) and Collins (1990).

the only point we want to make here is that it is possible. It is not possible to do this with mouth movements.[17]

Natural and Social Kinds

We can use the difference between social kinds and natural kinds to clarify the distinction between polimorphic actions, mimeomorphic actions, and (mere) behaviors. Both natural and social kind terms are social institutions in the sense that they have a self-referential component. But, as we have said, the self-referential component works differently in the two cases. In the case of money, there is nothing but self-reference—the reference is, as it were, "exhausted" by the self-reference. In the case of mountains, the term refers away from itself toward the physical world which is treated (within the institution at least), as existing independently of the reference. The continuing self-referential component of "mountain" consists of the criteria for classifying individuals as mountains. Nothing can be a model for anything in and of itself; a model of a mountain is what is collectively taken to be a model of a mountain, and that which is "Everest" is what is collectively taken to be "Everest."

Now let us put this distinction to work on the three things that humans do. Mere behaviors are recognized by means of natural kind terms—that is, mere behaviors are natural kinds.

Actions are social kinds; that is, actions are not just social institutions, they are social institutions in which self-reference exhausts the reference. Actions like "greeting," or "saying the Lord's Prayer," or "swinging a golf club" are like "money"; they exist because they are collectively constituted. Something is a greeting because it is collectively taken for a greeting; something is money because it is collectively taken to be money; something is a golf swing because it is collectively taken to be a golf swing. Actions are social kinds because communities are able to recognize their behavioral instantiations.

Polimorphic actions fit the above definition uniquely; a polimorphic action can never be specified by listing the behaviors in terms of which

17. It is, of course, just as easy to identify the printed letters "Y," "O," and "U" as the semaphor positions. The crucial comparison is between lip movements and arm movements.

it could be carried out. Thus one cannot specify a polimorphic action by means of natural kind terms.

A piece of behavior like a blink or other reflex is at the other pole of the dichotomy. A piece of behavior is part of the physical universe, and for certain purposes we can take such behaviors to be, like mountains, independent of our classifying activities.

Mimeomorphic actions are especially interesting because they have qualities belonging to both poles of the institution dichotomy. Because mimeomorphic actions are associated with fixed sets of behaviors, they can be identified in terms of natural kind terms. But a mimeomorphic action remains an action and can be looked upon, and identified as, a social kind; so, as an action (as opposed to a set of behaviors), its reference is exhausted by self-reference. Its behavioral instantiations are recognized by a collective, and this recognition is what makes this group of behaviors correspond to *this* rather than *that* mimeomorphic action.

Thus a Nick Faldo–type swing can be a natural kind term (as described in bodily movement terms by Nick Faldo's coach), and can be used to pick out a certain type of behavior from the other behaviors in the world around us. Note that picking out behaviors in this way is relative to cultures in the way that identifying mountains is, but not in the way that identifying polimorphic actions is. One does not have to be a member of the behaver's culture to identify the set of behaviors corresponding to a mimeomorphic action, but one does have to be a member of the culture to know which mimeomorphic action it corresponds to.

To sum up: The distinction between action and behavior maps onto the distinction between natural and social kinds. Polimorphic actions can be identified only by means of social kind terms. Mere behavior is solely a natural kind. Mimeomorphic actions can be identified by social kind terms, by natural kind terms, or by both. Behaviors carried out by machines that correspond to mimeomorphic actions can only be identified by means of natural kind terms, but may appear to constitute social kind terms.

Different cultures might have different taxonomies of human movements: For one culture a Nick Faldo–type swing behavior might be parsed into one sequence of movement descriptions, while for another culture a rather different set of movement categories might be used for capturing the same movement (just as some cultures might divide the world of precious and nonprecious stones differently than others do).

Nevertheless, it is characteristic of what we mean by behavior that different cultures can employ their different taxonomic resources for achieving the same effect: the repetition of the same (sequence of) behaviors. What we have just claimed about cultures also holds for machines, of course. A machine might mimic a human behavior—say a golf swing—without using any of the entrenched ways of parsing human behavior. It is able to repeat the behavior, although its (stored) description of the behavior is unlike any of the human descriptions.

Natural and Social Science

The difference between similarities of action and similarities of behavior can now be used to redescribe the difference between a natural and a social science. Imagine a group of "scientists" watching a group of "Saturnians." Saturnians do nothing all day except signal to each other in semaphor about the weather; the scientists do not know that. Saturnians know only 100 messages about the weather.

The scientists would have some chance of spotting regularities in the types of Saturnian behavior described above. They might first think that the Saturnians were "waving their upper limbs about." Then, after further study, they might note that the upper limb movements could be grouped into a eight different "positions" (given that angles between positions were rarely held for any length of time). Then some analyst (or computer program), might notice that the movements could be grouped into a limited set of sequences. Finally, some genius might notice that the sequences were correlated with the weather. The observers would thus have developed an observationally based science of Saturnian upper limb movements. It would include theories such as "the following sequence of upper limb movements is correlated with the appearance of the sun," and "such-and-such a sequence of upper limb movements is correlated with a hydrofluoric acid shower," and so forth. The observers will come to be able to predict what upper limb movement will come next by watching the horizon. Such a science has at least a chance of developing. It is a science of behavior made possible because the behavior of Saturnians is systematically related to their intended actions—making remarks about the weather. This, then, *pace* Weber,[18] is a science of intentional action made possible because, from the outside, it is indistinguishable from behavior. It may well be, of course, that the science does not develop for all the reasons that any science does not develop. Perhaps Saturnian Morse code is transmitted by tiny finger movements that earthly scientists do not have the visual acuity to detect; perhaps the Saturnians' movements are too rapid to see. All we are saying is that *one* reason for the science not to develop—the lack of order in behavior when it is motivated by polimorphic action—is not a problem.

Suppose, on the other hand, the Saturnians, not wishing to be "understood" by all and sundry, incorporated a complex code between their semaphoric movements and the symbols of their language that the movements represented. Let us say that those in the know learned this code every night from a randomly generated and secretly distributed "one-time" code sheet. The behavioral science of Saturnians would not then develop; the observers would never discover the ordering and the correlations of the arm movements.[19] Where any action is concerned, observers who do not understand the "code" that links behavior to action will, likewise, be unable to develop a predictive, observational science of the *behavior* found in the societies they observe.

In the case of polimorphic action, the "code" that links intention and behavior is complicated, cannot be set out, and can only be known through participation in the society being studied. There is nothing exotic about this claim. There is no more to it in principle than pointing out that one simply cannot recognize all the mouth movements associated with the utterance "you" unless one can recognize the sound "you" as a result of one's understanding of what is being said. This claim is given enormously strong empirical support by research into speech recognition by computers.

18. Gerth and Mills (1948).

19. What right do sociologists of science have to provide such a simplistic picture of science making? Even with nice ordered arm movements, the science might not develop because observation is not exact, because mistakes will be made, and because the scientists will argue; data must still be separated from noise. What is more, even if Saturnian arm movements were not systematically related to the weather, it is possible that the science *would* develop, so long as the scientists

The game of "Chinese whispers" gives a good indication of the differences discussed here. Imagine that the in-between people in a Chinese whispers chain contained only individuals who did not understand the language. We tried a small experiment to illustrate the point. Four graduate students at the University of Bath participated. None of the students knew semaphor, but they did know that in semaphor each arm was allowed to take one of eight positions. They were told a sequence of arm positions to learn and teach to a third party. They did not know what the arm positions signified. Nevertheless, the three letters Y-O-U were successfully transmitted through the chain.[20]

We then tried the same experiment with the French word "toi" using lip movements instead of arm movements. This time, when the final person in the chain was told that the word to be identified was a French word, she identified it incorrectly as "oui." The next experiment is to try Chinese whispers using skilled lip-readers working in a language they do not understand.

Sciences fail for two reasons (among many others). They fail because the things they try to correlate are randomly or chaotically associated in nature; long-range weather forecasting fails for this reason. Or they fail because the scientists do not understand the code. In the case of the social sciences, the necessary "code" cannot be understood except through participation.

Now we come to a crucial point. In the case of mimeomorphic actions, we could, in principle, have a purely observational, predictive science of behavior. It might be a lot easier and quicker to develop an understanding first, but in principle an outside observer could work out what counted as "the same" behaviors in a society and would have a chance of being right. Outsiders' and insiders' categories of sameness could match. Social science would then fulfill B. F. Skinner's dream and be a purely

---

were ingenious enough. The statements made here rest on a rather naive view of science as something that makes theory correspond with regularity found in nature, and we know it is not really like this. But what other resource have we if we want to speak of the possibility and impossibility of a science? The debate about the nature of the social sciences and the nature of methodology turns on this kind of thinking.

20. We did have some initial problems with mirror-image reversals.

"behavioral" science. In the case of polimorphic action, this is impossible.[21]

Two Kinds of Order

It is easy to overlook the distinction that has been made between orderly *behavior*—for which we can have a purely observational science—and orderly *action*—which requires the social scientist to gain a participant's comprehension if it is to be understood. It is easy to overlook this difference because we all have an enormous amount of low-level expertise in social affairs, and therefore we do not notice the extent to which we are skilled understanders even before we essay social scientific research.[22]

The two kinds of actions we talk about, polimorphic actions and mimeomorphic actions, give rise to *two kinds of order* in social life. Ordinary social life is full of order, but it is ordered polimorphic action, mutually understood through common enculturation. This is not the same as ordered behavior.

The matter is still more confusing, because at higher levels, orderly action can be organized within orderly behavior.[23] To give an example, under certain restaurant management regimes the manager of a restaurant might worry only about how many meals a waiter has served; as far as the manager is concerned, each meal served is like every other meal served. An observer watching the manager (even if not understanding), might spot the orderliness of the manager's behavior. Suppose the waiter hands in a "chit" every time a meal is served, and the manager gives the waiter a ten-dollar bill (as wages) every time ten meals are served. This

---

21. Note that it is not the case that one can *always* identify even a mimeomorphic action merely by observing behavior. The Saturnian case works because the scientist observers are making statistical generalizations. But a single action may fail; then the resulting behavior will not correspond to the intended action even though the actor intends it to correspond. (Perhaps one of the Saturnians is wearing a tight vest and cannot move its arms freely enough to execute its intentions.) Also, a single behavior might correspond to many actions.

22. This point will be dealt with again in a later chapter under the heading of "RAT."

23. The idea for the following example comes from Phil Agre's (1994) paper "The Grammar of Action." Agre is not responsible for the "types of action" element in the discussion.

correlation—between chits going one way and green pieces of paper going the other—could be spotted without any understanding of restaurants. But to understand what counted as the serving of a meal would be another matter altogether.

The distinction between polimorphic actions and mimeomorphic actions can be seen, as has been remarked, as a distinction between who (in principle) is able to see the order in it; who is able to make reasonable judgments of sameness about the behaviors they see. In the case of polimorphic action, only the enculturated can see sameness properly; in the case of mimeomorphic actions, nonenculturated observers might see it too. As it happens, there is hardly any situation on earth in which observers watching a society might really see regularities of behavior without any understanding, because on earth mimeomorphic actions are nearly always intimately mixed with polimorphic actions, and this would confound the sort of science of behavior that works on Saturn. It is only in strange and unusual circumstances that a science of behavior could really work.[24]

24. Surprisingly, many economists believe all action is of this type.

3

Morphicity: What the Action Is

There are polimorphic actions and mimeomorphic actions. Mimeomorphic actions are actions that we either seek to *or are content to* carry out in pretty much the same way, in terms of behavior, on different occasions. Polimorphic actions are all the rest.[1]

For our purpose, we are going to use the term "behavior" in a special sense. In ordinary language, as well as in the philosophical literature, behavior is roughly equivalent to "internally produced movement or change."[2] Understood in this way, human actions are a species of behavior, other species of behavior being the behavior of machines, animals, or plants. It is more useful in this context to define the notion of "behavior" as any sequence of bodily movements. Behaviors are what observers see people doing; they can be described by mapping bodily movements onto space–time coordinates.[3] Actions, on the other hand

1. In some sense we are engaged in the phenomenology of action, which is a step beyond the realm of issues traditionally addressed by the philosophy of action. The dominant tradition in the philosophy of action has been concerned with issues such as the logical structure of action sentences, freedom of the will, the nature of intentions, the causal or noncausal relation between intentions and actions, the differences between actions and happenings, and the viability of "folk theory" in describing, explaining, and predicting human actions. The almost exclusive focus on these problems has left other philosophical questions concerning actions underanalyzed. We are thinking here of the tradition in which the works of Anscombe (1979), Chisholm (1970), Danto (1973), Davidson (1982), and Goldman (1970) are seminal.

2. Cf. Dretske (1991), p. 3.

3. Our definition of behavior does not obviously cover "behaviors" such as calculating "in one's head" where no bodily movements are visible. Nevertheless, as has been shown elsewhere (Collins 1990), such "mental" actions can be

are, always associated in one way or another with an intention (even though the actor may not be consciously aware of the intention from moment to moment). Therefore, for us, an action is the behavior plus the intention. An outside observer may not always see the difference between a piece of behavior that is the counterpart of an action and one that is not, but it is clear that it makes sense to talk of such a difference. Of course, in the way we use the term, action also involves a relationship to a form of life.

We can now say something about the difference between our two generic types of actions—polimorphic actions and mimeomorphic actions.

Polimorphic Actions

Each of the generic types of action has subspecies. The simplest way to understand polimorphic actions is to note that in the case of many types of actions, the *same action* can be carried out by an indefinite number of *different behaviors*. For example, paying money can be done by passing metal or paper tokens, writing a check, offering a plastic card and signing a chit, and so forth, and each of these can be done in an open-ended variety of ways. At the same time, the *same* piece of *behavior* may be the instantiation of many *different actions*. For example, signing one's name might be the action of paying money, or it might be agreeing to a divorce, the final flourish of a suicide note, or a specimen signature for the bank.

Polimorphic actions are "rule bound" in the sense that it is usually clear when they are being done the wrong way. For example, there are wrong ways of doing even so ill-defined a thing as going for a walk. One

---

understood as being associated with what can be thought of as internalized behaviors. Thus if one thinks of a child's action of adding (on the fingers) as being the coordination of chanting and finger movements, we may think of mental arithmetic as being the same thing done in "the mind's eye." The analysis of both "mental actions" and actions that involve no movement, such as pretending to be a statue, is the same, but to sort out their conceptual structure it is easier to think about actions that do have a counterpart in observable behavior. (One of the reasons we use the term "behavior" rather than "movement" is because a subset of the actions that we analyze involve no intentional movement.)

way to do it wrong in many societies would be to brush against others on the sidewalk. Though polimorphic actions are rule bound, it is not possible to provide a recipe for doing them the right way that could be followed by someone who did not already understand the society in which they are embedded—there are too many context-dependent possibilities.

All types of (formative intentional) actions that are *not* mimeomorphic actions are "polimorphic actions." The presence of variability in behavioral instantiation is characteristic of polimorphic actions. The variability with which an action of type "a" can be realized is thus part of what the action of type "a" means for the agent. Polimorphic actions are characterized by essential variability in the behaviors with which they are executed. Polimorphic actions are characterized by the fact that they usually involve varying behavior to carry out the same action in relation to a situation. The prefix "poly" connotes "manyness," referring to the many behaviors that must correspond to a polimorphic action, but we have used the pun "poli" to connote that the appropriate behavioral shape of such an action has to be determined by reference to the society (polis). Thus, polimorphic actions are both many-shaped and take their shape from society.

If we separate the variations in situation from the choice of behavioral responses, we can distinguish four types of actions, three of which are polimorphic. There are *open polimorphic actions* in which both situation and response are open; there are *occasioned polimorphic actions* in which only the situation is open; and there are *playful polimorphic actions* in which only the behavioral response is open. In the fourth class of actions both situation and behavioral response are determinate; these are *mimeomorphic actions*. We now look briefly at each type of polimorphic action.[4]

Open Polimorphic Actions: Love Letter Writing

We take writing love letters as an example of an *open polimorphic action.* Writing a love letter is an action such that different ways of carrying out

4. We adopt the convention of italicizing the first references to subspecies of action in each section, since each subspecies consists of three or four words. The italics distinguish subspecies from qualifying adjectives.

the action are not only possible but desirable. In fact, the difficulty (for some writers) of writing love letters over a prolonged period of time (and to the same beloved person), is to invent ever new ways of expressing one's love and affection that are still meaningful. A love letter that was an exact reproduction of an earlier one would be considered an insult or joke. Of course we can imagine circumstances under which an exact reproduction would still function as a love letter—say, where the beloved asked for such reproduction as a token of love—but these are special circumstances. Usually, writing a love letter will be a highly contextualized action, relating to the stylistic conventions of the times (courtly love, the restrained formality of Victorian society, the new freedoms of the 1960s), the form of life of the participants (gentlepersons, the Amish, punks), and the setting of the letters within the series of earlier letters and the major happenings in the world (periods of prosperity, major natural disasters, wars).

Though love letter writers are expected to be creative, it would be a misunderstanding to take an "open" choice to mean an "unbounded" choice. The creativity is bounded by conventions; there is a difference between a love letter and, say, a business letter. But these conventions— the conventions that keep society ordered—are conventions that constrain *actions*. Conventions that constrain *actions* put nothing like same the constraint on *behaviors* (as we use the term). To repeat the crucial point, to remain within the convention of the action "love letter writing" requires creativity in behavior. Love letter writing, then, requires an imaginative response to open-ended, changing circumstances, and it requires creativity within the bounds of convention; both context and response are open.

Occasioned Polimorphic Actions: Voting

A good example of an *occasioned polimorphic action* is voting. Imagine a system in which members of parliament are asked to vote on bills that come before the house by pressing one of three buttons. The three buttons signify "for," "against," and "abstain." Imagine, if possible, that these parliamentarians vote with their conscience every time. The members' behavioral repertoire is severely constrained in this case—they can do one of only three things—but they respond with one of these three behaviors to an open ended environment consisting of the bills that come before them and the ever-changing world to which the parliamentary debates are a response or a contribution. An outside observer who did not understand the nature of a parliament or the world in which it was set would be unable to predict members' voting patterns even though there were only three possibilities. Thus even the identical behavior—say, pressing the "for" button—might comprise entirely different actions each time. Pressing the "for" button might be voting to, say, legalize abortion, to outlaw abortion, or to raise taxes on chocolate.

To summarize, *occasioned polimorphic actions* happen when a limited set of behaviors is used to respond in a meaningful way to an open context.[5]

Playful Polimorphic Actions: Relieving Tedium, Expressing Individuality
A typical example of a *playful polimorphic action* occurs when assembly-line workers vary the way they manage a repetitive tedious job, not as a meaningful response to an open environment, and not because variation is needed to do the job properly, but because they are trying to relieve the tedium of the task without loss of efficiency. Behavioral variations of this sort might well be random; they are not socially embedded.[6]

5. When one types a letter, one has a limited choice of keys to press. Therefore, for all letters of finite length, one is choosing from what one might think of as a finite (albeit very large) choice of combinations of key presses. Why, then, are not all typed letters instances of occasioned polimorphic actions like the voting case where the choice was limited to one of a set of button pressings? The answer is that while all button pressings are potential votings, not all combinations of key presses are potential letter writings—in fact most are not: they are just nonsense. To understand which of the set of all combinations of key presses comprise letter writings, one has first to understand the society in which letter writing is taking place, and that is why the behavioral choice is not predetermined as it is in the case of voting by pressing buttons.

The fact that each of the "terminal actions" involved in writing a letter—pressing a key—comprises one choice from a limited range does not affect the argument, for key pressing is not letter writing. Key pressing is an action embedded within the action of letter writing.

6. Though in practice, playfulness at work is probably more ritualized than random, it does not effect the conceptual distinction we are making. There may be few pure examples of the types of actions we describe to be found in the world

Playful polimorphic actions fill up the logical space we have created by separating behavioral responses from the context in which they take place. It is characterized by a limited context and an open-ended repertoire of behaviors.

A variant of playful polimorphic actions is personalized action. An example would be the deliberate use of handwriting, as opposed to typing, in the production of a letter. In writing by hand, the writer introduces variation into symbol formation so as to reveal that the origin of the text was not a machine, but the variations are not meaningful. Here the variation from letter to letter and word to word is a way of symbolically expressing individuality, care, and personal effort.

While then, such actions are responses to social situations (whereas the previous example of the bored production-line worker was a response to an individual, psychological need), the actual variation in the formation of the symbols is not socially meaningful—that there is variation is meaningful, but the particular variations are not. Playful polimorphic actions, in their personalized variant, are formative actions, because their meaning is rooted in our forms of life, but they are, paradoxically, an institutionalized way of expressing individuality.[7]

Figure 3.1 shows the relationship of the three types of polimorphic actions and of mimeomorphic actions.

Mimeomorphic Actions

The starting point for understanding mimeomorphic actions is to think of them as actions where, by contrast with polimorphic actions, we attempt to maintain a one-to-one mapping between our actions and observable behaviors. As in the execution of all actions, we may intend to execute mimeomorphic actions in a certain way, but this is not necessarily what we accomplish. Nevertheless, the proper description of the type of action is informed by our intention to do things in the same way

---

as we know it. The point is, however, to describe exhaustively possible types of actions and then to break down those we encounter into their components.

7. Compare this concept to shooting the Archduke Ferdinand; this is not an institutionalized way of expressing individuality and is not, therefore, a formative action.

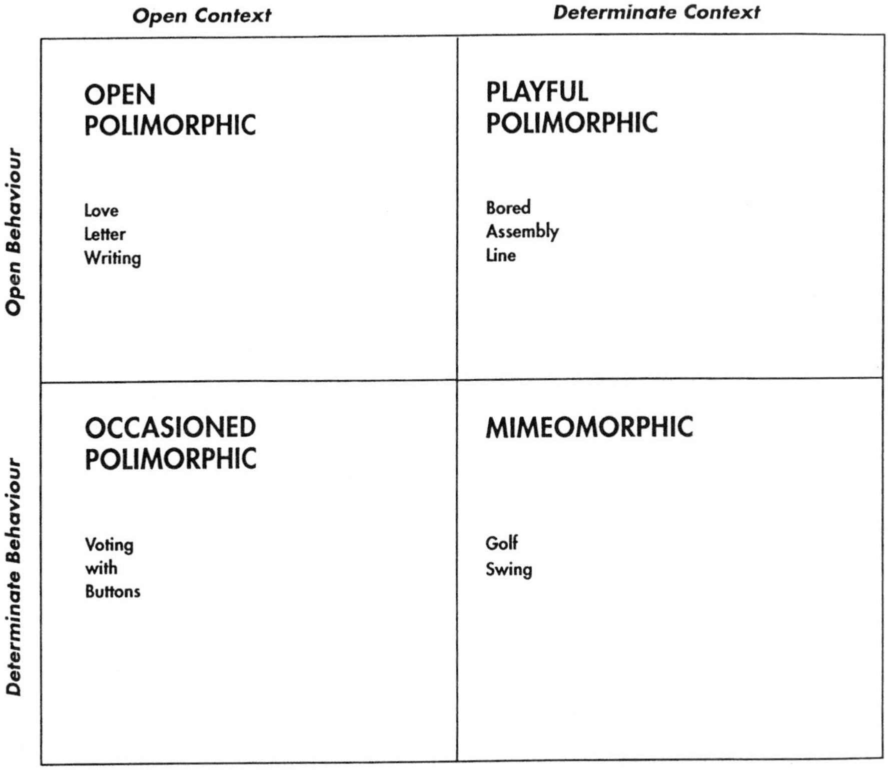

	Open Context	**Determinate Context**
Open Behaviour	**OPEN POLIMORPHIC** Love Letter Writing	**PLAYFUL POLIMORPHIC** Bored Assembly Line
Determinate Behaviour	**OCCASIONED POLIMORPHIC** Voting with Buttons	**MIMEOMORPHIC** Golf Swing

Figure 3.1
Polimorphic actions and mimeomorphic actions.

(or, as we will come to see, by the envelope of our indifference to exactly how we carry out an action).

We call such actions *mimeomorphic* because the behaviors associated with the action can be copied from previous instances. Whereas polimorphic actions are both many-shaped and take their shape from society, mimeomorphic actions are same-shaped and take their shape from previous examples of the same action.

Four types of mimeomorphic actions can be assembled by combining two of their properties. Every mimeomorphic action must be more or less *special* or *casual* and it must be *singular* or *disjunctive*. The four types of mimeomorphic actions comprise the four combinations of these two dichotomies though the casual–special dimension is more of a continuum than a dichotomy.

Special Singular Mimeomorphic Actions: Swinging a Golf Club

When one swings a golf club—let us say one is hitting balls at a driving range—one seeks to produce (in most cases) a specific and fixed bodily movement every time. One puts one's feet at a certain distance from one another, bends one's knees, keeps one's left arm straight, holds the club with one's hands overlapping in a certain way, lowers one's head such that one's eyes remain fixed on the ball throughout the swinging movement, and so forth. The club is lifted into the air and swung back as the upper body turns, again in a specific and fixed fashion. The downswing starts with a sideways movement of the knees. The learner is told how to position and move almost every part of the body, from heels and toes to the top of the head, the aim being to develop the ability, first to execute these movements optimally, and then to reproduce the optimum movements time after time. As golfers know, it is hard to learn to produce the optimum movements even once, but it is still harder to reproduce them reliably. Even the best golfers in the world spend much of their time with their coaches adjusting and "grooving" their swing when it drifts away from the optimal.

In the modern game the same philosophy extends through all the golf clubs (except the putter) that are used to strike the ball. The golfer is advised not to try to hit the ball more softly when the target is at a lesser distance, but instead to choose a shorter, less powerful club, which, when swung in the same way, will have the effect of projecting the ball less far. Thus, for instance, a 7-iron in the hands of a good player hits the ball 150 yards and an 8-iron 140 yards. The experienced player who has mastered this standardized way of hitting the ball has more difficulty with shots that are "between clubs"—say 145 yards in length—than with a normal shot. To send the ball this distance, other things being equal, the golfer will have to hit unusually hard or unusually soft. Professional golfers who have played a bad shot in televised tournament often explain by saying that the shot was "between clubs." It is worth noting that this problem does not arise for the poor player, who is not yet able to hit shots in a mimeomorphic way. For the poor player a 150 yard shot is just as hard as a 145 yard shot.

What we have so far said about golf applies to today's game played according to today's coaching conventions. This coaching philosophy would lead the player to carry a separate club for each distance. It has not always been thus, as the following quotation illustrates:

Golfers weren't restricted to 14 clubs until the late 1930s. In any case, in earlier years, no one even thought of carrying such a vast quantity. Open Champions around the turn of the century regarded 7 to 10 clubs as the norm. Between the wars, all this changed dramatically. Rightly or wrongly, top professionals decided that it is far more difficult to be consistent when you have to vary your swing pace, and alter your clubface position at impact by manipulating it with the hands. They felt it was far easier to repeat a standard swing. Some of them began to carry, not 14 clubs, but quantities soaring into the 20's. (Hobbs 1991, p. 59)

It is clear, then, that before the interwar period swinging a golf club was not the sort of mimeomorphic action it is now; golfers were not trying to "groove their swings" in the same way.[8] One might say that the "morphicity" of the golf swing has changed.[9]

Special Disjunctive Mimeomorphic Actions: Expert Golf Club Swinging
As golfers become more expert, they learn to reduce the variations in bodily movement as far as possible but, once they have mastered this, they may learn certain specific variations of the swing. For example, slight variations of position of hands and feet can result in side spin being imparted to the ball. The novice golfer tries desperately to eliminate unwanted side spin, such as gives rise to the dreaded "slice," by fixing the position of hands and feet, but the expert may introduce deliberate variations of stance to produce controlled spin so as to fly the ball around trees or away from dangers. Let us say that middle-ranking golfers can

8. They may have thought of their swings as a very complicated disjunctive mimeomorphic actions.
9. Jenkins (1994) has brought the analysis of the golf swing up to date. He finds that there are golf swing "paradigms" and paradigm revolutions. At one time what was generally thought to be the proper swing was modeled on that of Ben Hogan, at a later date on that of Jack Nicklaus, and more recently on Nick Faldo's swing.

hit three types of shot: the straight shot, the left to right shot, and the right to left shot. Imagine such a golfer standing with a tree between him- or herself and the target. If the tree is tall and the bulk of it is to the golfer's left, then he or she will go around the right-hand side by hitting a right to left shot. If the tree is tall but the bulk is to the golfer's right, then a left to right shot is called for. If the tree is short, then he or she will hit a straight shot over the top. Where the circumstances are such that the choice can be predicted, this is a *disjunctive mimeomorphic action*. We call it "disjunctive" because the actor has to choose to execute the action in one or other of a set of mutually exclusive ways, each of which is itself a mimeomorphic action.

Whether to describe this three-choice golf swing as a disjunctive mimeomorphic action or three individual singular mimeomorphic actions is a matter for the analyst; both descriptions are correct. Because actions are embedded within other actions, there are always choices of this kind to be made by the analyst. All *disjunctive mimeomorphic actions* could be described as combinations of individual *singular mimeomorphic actions*.

It is important to note the difference between disjunctive mimeomorphic actions and *occasioned polimorphic actions* (our example was voting with buttons). In this case, as we have just said, three separate singular mimeomorphic actions can be thought of as one combined disjunctive mimeomorphic action. In the voting case discussed above, a button pressing, considered on its own, is a mimeomorphic action. But the three possible mimeomorphic actions that make up the voter's choice do not constitute a disjunctive mimeomorphic action—they constitute a polimorphic action, because the choice between them is socially situated. In the golf case, the choice is predictable from the outside. Assuming the golfer is trying to do his or her best in terms of the game as it is currently played, rather than, say, "showing off," the shot can in principle be predicted from the relative position of the ball and the tree. That one is predictable and the other is not has to do with the openness of the context in the case of voting and the closedness in the case of our golf example, where the three choices of shot correspond to three well-defined and specifiable situations.

Another example of a disjunctive mimeomorphic action is chair spraying. Imagine a Taylorist assembly line in which workers are trained to spray chairs in the most efficient manner for each shape of chair. Let there be three models of chair passing along the assembly line in random order. The movements that the chair sprayer makes will be one of three mimeomorphic actions, the relevant mimeomorphic action being chosen to match the model of chair passing at that moment. The universe of chairs is exhaustive—there are no in-between cases—and the sprayer's behavior would be predictable.

But what if there are in-between cases? The problem for the golfer is easily seen. A really good golfer might break down the "obstructing-tree-situation" into many more than three cases. In fact, for a really good golfer there is a "continuous" scale of possibilities. Such a golfer would try to put more or less side spin on the ball, depending on just how far the tree obtrudes into the line of the shot, and therefore on how far the flight path of the ball has to be "bent." The really good golfer's rule about how much spin he or she would like to put on the ball can be expressed as a function of the extent to which the tree protrudes into the line of the straight shot. This is still mimeomorphic action because in every case the degree of spin preferred by the golfer could be predicted in advance, even though every case cannot be anticipated; what can be anticipated is the full range of possibilities and the full range of eventualities that would lead to the choice of a shot from the range.[10]

The golfer, choosing from a range of degrees of side spin according to the extent of intrusion of the tree into the proposed flight of the ball, is responding to the environment (through visually mediated "feedback"). A more obvious case of feedback is, say, a person polishing a panel of a car. The person keeps the polishing rag in contact with the surface of the

10. In Collins (1990) a "record-and-playback" chair sprayer was discussed. The initial recording of the human chair sprayer's movements is a matter of recording a continuous function. Furthermore, the example allows for any number of different chair shapes to be recorded and played back. As the number becomes large, the difference between discrete and continuous rules gets lost. To put this another way, no applicable function is truly continuous, because the world is not truly continuous.

paintwork by pressing down and allowing the shape of the metal to guide the muscles. This is still *disjunctive mimeomorphic action,* because, once more, the range is understood in advance and the function that accounts for the response to the environment is understood in advance. In this case the full set of movements that might be described cannot be predicted in advance because one cannot predict the shape of the panels of cars yet to be designed. Nevertheless, one can predict the envelope of shapes and thus the function. Or, to put this the other way, it is only to the extent that one cannot predict the range of shapes that one cannot say that car polishing is mimeomorphic. If someone starts designing car panels with sharp-edged troughs or spikes, normal car polishing will break down, and something new will have to be invented.

Casual Singular Mimeomorphic Actions: Telephoning One's Mother from Home

To telephone one's mother from home, one must engage in a mimeomorphic action. If one has, say, a push-button phone, one must pick up the handset and press the same sequence of buttons in the same order every time one telephones. Therefore one is trying to execute that action—telephoning mother—with the same behavior on each occasion. Notice, however, that this action is different from swinging a golf club, in that we are not trying to standardize the position of other parts of our body. We do not need to keep a stiff left arm; we do not need to bend our knees or place our feet at shoulder width; we do not need to keep our head still; we do not need to grip the phone in just such and such a way; nor need we press the buttons with just such and such a pressure or tempo. While there are limits outside of which our movements must not stray, the envelope is much wider than in the case of golf. We do not need to concentrate or undergo lengthy training in order to remain within the limits of telephone manipulation that count as skilled, nor do we care whether we press the buttons and hold the phone in just the same way on different occasions or in countless different ways. In short, whereas in the case of the golf swing our attention is all on the matter of standardizing our movements as far as possible, in the case of telephone dialing we are *indifferent* to the range of movements that lies within the envelope of acceptable behavior—that is, the range of movements that will amount to calling up the relevant number.

This is a *casual action*, as opposed to a *special mimeomorphic action*, because the mimeomorphic character of the action is not marked, as in the case of a special mimeomorphic action, by our preference for the same behavioral instantiation each time, but by our indifference to how the action is behaviorally accomplished (within limits). This indifference is made evident by the following observation: We would not care if the action was carried out every time with identical bodily movements. It is for this reason that it makes sense to call such actions mimeomorphic even though our attention is not focused on maximizing identity of behavior. The contrast with polimorphic actions is still clear: Both polimorphic actions and *casual mimeomorphic actions* involve variety in the behavioral instantiation of actions, but in polimorphic actions the variations are meaningful and cannot be collapsed into the same behaviors every time, whereas in a casual mimeomorphic action they are not meaningful and they can be collapsed without loss. To put this another way, as opposed to the case of polimorphic actions, the variability with which casual mimeomorphic actions can be realized is *not* a part of what the action means for the agent.

As we will go on to see, even special mimeomorphic actions have an element of casual mimeomorphic action about them, so that the difference is one of degree, though the difference in intention is often very clear, as in the telephone and golf swing cases. Degrees of variability in the behavioral instantiation of an action exist, as it were, phenomenologically: they exist for the agent and they are an objective feature of the agent's community, but they do not map straightforwardly onto degrees of variation in the physically observable features of the action.

Casual Disjunctive Mimeomorphic Actions: Telephoning
In the case of telephoning one's mother from home, one is always using the same phone and always calling the same number. In the case of telephoning in general, one calls from a variety of phones—pay phones with buttons, phones with dials—and calls a variety of numbers. Each action of telephoning is a mimeomorphic action that is designed for the

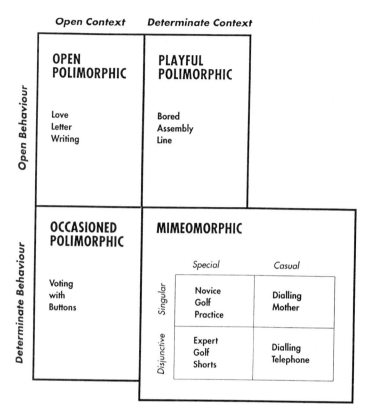

Figure 3.2
Seven types of actions and their relationship.

particular phone and for the particular number. For each of our interactions with telephones, what we said about telephoning one's mother is true, but each case is fitted to the particular context which determines, in a predictable way, the envelope of behaviors that make up the mimeomorphic action. Once more, as in the expert golf swing or the chair-spraying example, a set of mimeomorphic actions—in this case a set of telephonings—is assembled to form a higher level disjunctive mimeomorphic action. In this case, however, the higher level choice is between casual mimeomorphic actions, so this is an example of a casual disjunctive mimeomorphic action.

All seven types of morphicity of actions are set out in figure 3.2.

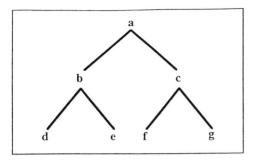

Figure 3.3
Traveling to London by train.

Diagrammatic Representation of Actions

Many relationships between actions are better understood and more easy to analyze with the use of diagrams. We use open and closed triangles to represent actions, the width of the base representing the degree of freedom of the behavioral instantiation.

Polimorphic Actions: Open Triangles
In what we will call an *action tree*, higher nodes stand for types of actions that are realized lower down the tree by more precisely defined action types. Thus for instance "traveling to London on the early morning train" (labeled as "d" in figure 3.3), falls under "traveling to London by train" "b," which in turn falls under "traveling to London" "a."

Of course the tree structure is no more then an idealization of relations between types of actions, since a given action can often be specified in more than just two ways (e.g., writing a love letter can be specified in an endless number of ways), so the bifurcation of figure 3.3 is too simple. What is more, there may be many more levels to the tree. We will analyze trees, and the paths through them that actors adopt, in greater detail below. In the meantime we will introduce a diagrammatic shorthand for the complexities of an action tree. In this convention, we collapse all the levels and represent the open-ended branching of the tree by an open triangle. Thus a given action type with its possible realizations will be represented as in figure 3.4. Here, "a" stands for a type of action such

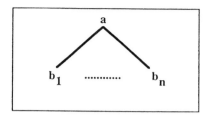

Figure 3.4
Collapsed action tree.

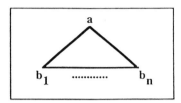

Figure 3.5
Mimeomorphic action represented by a closed triangle.

that it can be carried out in an indefinite number of ways and such that the ways "b1" to "bn" in which the action "a" can be carried out, are significant for the actor and/or his or her community. The actor chooses one way of carrying out action "a" on a given occasion, that is, selects one possibility from the *domain of choice* "b1" to "bn."

Mimeomorphic Action: Closed Triangles

The actions of swinging a golf club (on a driving range without trees in the way), or Taylorist chair spraying do not have open action trees. To begin to develop a representation, we take a casual singular mimeomorphic action such as telephoning one's mother, symbolized by a closed triangle as in figure 3.5. Here "a" stands for a type of action such that actors (or their community, or both) *do not care about* which way, "b1" to "bn," they carry out action "a," so long as it falls within the triangular envelope of possibilities. The actor happens to carry out the action "a" in some way on a given occasion, but takes no interest in which particular element from "b1" to "bn" was used, or in varying the instantiations of this action. Thus in this case, "b1" to "bn" do not constitute an open

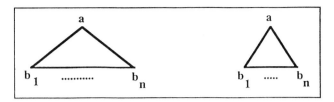

Figure 3.6
Mimeomorphic actions with different envelopes of behavior.

domain of choice, but rather an *area of tolerance* or *indifference* to which the actor does not attend.

Casual and Special Mimeomorphic Actions: Width of Triangles
Moving downward in an action tree amounts to fixing more and more aspects of how the higher action type is to be carried out on a given occasion. At the branching nodes, choices must be made, either explicitly and consciously, or else implicitly and unconsciously. Put differently, we might say that the downward movement fixes more and more parameters of an action. Focusing for the moment only on mimeomorphic actions, let us imagine ourselves constructing a rough and ready list of the things that are important in our examples of *special* and *casual mimeomorphic actions,* golf club swinging and telephoning. In the case of the golf swing, the list would include almost every part of our body, and the specification for the movement of each of these parts of our body would be narrow. In the case of telephoning, a few movements of the arms and hands would be specified within wide limits. The degree of constraint can be represented by narrow and wide triangles, as in figure 3.6. The more parameters of a mimeomorphic action are fixed—the smaller the area of tolerance or indifference—the narrower the triangle.

This kind of representation helps us to understand the interplay of the intentional description of action and the physical description. In the case of special mimeomorphic actions, of which the learner's golf swing is a paradigm, the actor is attempting to collapse the triangle entirely—to eliminate variation altogether. And this is what it feels like! From the point of view of an actor, then, a special mimeomorphic action is an attempt to collapse the triangle into a straight line, as in figure 3.7. But, described in terms of what an outside observer would see of our rough

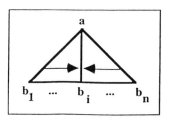

Figure 3.7
Ideal type of a special mimeomorphic action.

list of physical and physiological parameters, the learner's triangle would be far more open because learners are not very successful at collapsing the triangle. For an outside observer, the degree of physical variation in the swing of a learner, and in the swing of a professional "clowning about" and imitating a learner, would be similar, but the intentions would be quite different. In the first case, the learner would be engaged in special mimeomorphic actions (though not very successfully); in the second case the professional would be engaged in the action "clowning about," which is polimorphic action.[11] Thus in terms of physical parameters, two actions that fall on the opposite sides of our major dichotomy look the same; once more we see the difficulty of doing social science "from the outside" unless there is nothing going on but mimeomorphic action.

Now suppose the learner succeeds and becomes a professional who is having a good day on the practice ground, so that as far as he or she, or a passing observer, or a watching golfing coach is concerned, the triangle has been collapsed. Even then, the triangle is still open within other frames of reference. As we remarked earlier, within the framework of the person whose dog is hit by one shot but not by another, or within the framework of an engineer with a high-speed camera and a micrometer, two golf swings that seem identical to the golfer will look different. Thus if one attends even to successfully executed special mimeomorphic actions within the right frame of reference, one will see that the straight line is really a narrow triangle, as in figure 3.8. Once again, that it is possible

11. Probably it is a playful polimorphic action because the variations in the behavioral instantiation are deliberately opened up, but the variations would be nearer to random than meaningful.

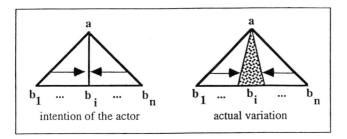

Figure 3.8
Close-up view of a special mimeomorphic action.

for an actor from one community to see two actions as the same, whereas an actor from another community would not, is a matter of the respective areas of tolerance that are used to define sameness.

To sum up, in the case of special mimeomorphic actions, the actor is attempting to collapse the triangle, while the actor in casual mimeomorphic actions is indifferent to what happens within the base of the triangle. Should the triangle collapse, and the action be carried out in what might appear to be the identical way every time, the actor would not care. (We would not care if, every time we phoned our mothers, we had our feet, knees, head, etc., in exactly the same position, or whether we always pressed the buttons with the same force and tempo. We would not even notice should this be the case.) It might be said, then, that special mimeomorphic actions and casual mimeomorphic actions merge into one another, for even in special mimeomorphic actions the actor is indifferent to variations that do not belong to the frame of reference of the activity in question (the golfer is indifferent to the differences noticed by the dog owner and the engineer.) As we will see, the similarities between all kinds of mimeomorphic actions are, for many purposes, more important than the differences; the differences, however, reflect our experience as actors and observers.

Playful Polimorphic Actions Revisited
At this point it is worth returning to *playful polimorphic actions*. Playful polimorphic actions occupy an interestingly ambiguous position within the scheme; this makes the significance of the major division still more clear. We have located playful polimorphic actions on the polimorphic

action side of the major dichotomy because the actor would not be indifferent to a collapse of the triangle into a straight line. The unusual thing is that the actor's concern is not with the meaningfulness of the various positions within the triangle that represent different behavioral instantiations of the action, but solely with keeping the triangle opened up—to relieve tedium. The only meaningfulness is in the width of the triangle, not the structure within it; in this, playful polimorphic actions are unlike the other two categories of polimorphic actions. The meaninglessness of the internal structure of playful polimorphic actions makes them mimeomorphic actions more than polimorphic actions. That is that is why they are an interesting interstitial case.

Compare playful polimorphic actions with occasioned polimorphic actions (e.g., voting with buttons). In the latter case, the width of the triangle is very narrow in terms of most frames of reference. Thus in our voting example only one of three choices is available. Nevertheless, the meaning of the structure within that narrow triangle of choices is crucial.

Disjunctive Mimeomorphic Actions: Divided Triangles

In *disjunctive mimeomorphic actions* the behavior is related to a determinate set of contexts such that one mimeomorphic action is required for each prespecified (or potentially prespecificable), situation.[12] Our clearest example of this was chair spraying on a Taylorist assembly line. We represent disjunctive mimeomorphic actions as a closed triangle divided into sections as in figure 3.9. Each line of the triangle represents one of the ways in which the action will be executed.

One might say that the research program of artificial intelligence (at least, the program that preceded neural nets and so forth), involves

12. "Potentially prespecifiable" includes cases where the actor (or delegate) is provided with an algorithm for recognizing the situation even though the exact constituents of the situation may not have been thought through in advance. For example, an algorithm of this sort is used by skilled people who have to drill holes in plates. Skilled hole drillers know that the torque experienced by a drill bit increases just before the bit breaks completely through. (When the residue of the material being drilled becomes so thin that the forward pressure of the drill distorts the material, the torque will momentarily increase.) They know they should relieve pressure on the drill at this moment. This feature of drilling is used in the design of machines to drill holes automatically in surgical settings such as automated ear surgery. (Annemiek Nelis provided this example.)

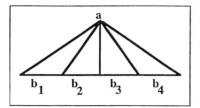

Figure 3.9
Disjunctive mimeomorphic action.

making machines that do the behavioral equivalent of more and more ramified trees of disjunctive mimeomorphic actions. Those who believe in "strong AI" think that all actions are ramified trees of disjunctive mimeomorphic actions. We would say that such people confuse densely ramified *disjunctive mimeomorphic actions* with polimorphic actions. They think that as a triangle becomes more and more densely filled with alternate paths, it becomes indistinguishable from an open triangle.[13]

Actions Embedded within One Another

Every mimeomorphic action in part realizes a higher action type that need not itself be a mimeomorphic action; in other words, as we have already mentioned, mimeomorphic actions can be embedded in polimorphic actions. For instance, swinging a golf club in part realizes the higher action type "playing golf," an action that is not mimeomorphic. Playing golf includes actions such as negotiating with the caddie, estimating distances, judging wind conditions, considering one's opponent's strengths and weaknesses, "gamesmanship," and so forth. All of these are polimorphic actions (though they may each contain components that are mimeomorphic actions). If the sequence of realizations is followed high enough, all actions are embedded in polimorphic actions, because all actions are embedded within societies.

13. Some of the arguments about the Turing test are about the distinguishability or otherwise of these two kinds of actions as they reveal themselves in conversation. The person in John Searle's "Chinese Room" is engaged in pure *disjunctive mimeomorphic actions*. These are distinguishable from polimorphic actions if the appropriate questions are asked (Collins 1990, chaps. 13 and 14). See also Collins (1996), where the Turing test is replaced with the "editing test."

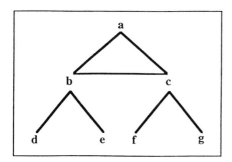

Figure 3.10
An impossible action tree.

Though mimeomorphic actions can be embedded in polimorphic actions, polimorphic actions cannot be embedded in mimeomorphic actions. In terms of our diagrammatic representation, figure 3.10 is impossible. For action "a" to be a mimeomorphic action, the agent should be indifferent to how "a" is carried out in terms of behavior, as long as it falls within the area of tolerance. And this can only mean that the indifference should go all the way down, that is, "b" and "c" should be closed as well. If "b" or "c" were open, the way that "b" or "c" was carried out would be a matter of concern to the actor, and this would mean that the way "a" was executed would be of concern, because "a" is executed through the execution of "b" or "c."

As we said, one can have mimeomorphic actions within polimorphic actions. This is because the variations of behavior through which the action is executed are given their contextual meaning at the higher level of the embedding action.

Nearly all polimorphic action trees have mimeomorphic action embedded within them. In many cases, as one goes down an action tree, the ratio of mimeomorphic actions to polimorphic actions will increase, and nearly all action trees will terminate in "mimeomorphic actions."[14] Thus,

14. To anticipate our major argument, because mimeomorphic actions can be delegated to entities that do not understand contexts but will work according to plans, the lower levels of action trees can often be delegated to tools. A frequent mistake is to try to delegate too far up the action tree. To put this another way, the mistake is to shift the locus of control from the human tool user to the tool.

nearly all actions, including polimorphic actions, are, as it were, assembled out of mimeomorphic actions. An assembly of mimeomorphic actions might, then, constitute either a polimorphic action or a disjunctive mimeomorphic action; it depends on the kind of choice that is being made at the higher level. Note that this does not mean that a polimorphic action can be reduced to an assembly of mimeomorphic actions; it is the way the mimeomorphic actions are arranged and chosen that constitutes a polimorphic action.[15]

See Lipscombe (1989) for an analysis of this problem in the context of medical expert systems.

To save possible confusion, consider the following. Suppose a naive observer watches a virtuoso piano player. He or she sees only a sequence of key presses. The observer might reproduce these in a mimeomorphic way, believing that he or she has reproduced the action. The reproduced action, however, would be characterized by the novice's indifference to the exact way each key was pressed, since he or she will think that this was also a matter of indifference to the pianist. Virtuosi, or skilled critics, however, would be able to see the difference. The naive observer would have believed they were watching an action that could be described "externally," as one might say. The virtuoso or the skilled critic would know that this was not so. But replace the novice observer with a device for recording and playing back the piano key pressings "exactly" as they were played—for example, think of a pianola roll being played back on a modern recording piano. Surely then the polimorphic action is being reproduced by a device that cannot respond to social context! But the virtuoso pianist must play according to the response of the audience and the mood of the times; if not, there would be no need for live concerts. A musical performance is like a love letter (see below). To replay a pianola roll is like rereading a love letter. To substitute the roll for the live performance is like sending the same letter over and over again.

This way of putting the matter shows how the role of piano playing might correspond to the role of language in a Turing-like test of the pianist. Novice piano playing, like novice (Chinese Room) language speaking, is generally mimeomorphic, whereas virtuoso piano playing is not. (But not all expert activity is polimorphic—see chapter 5).

15. There is an interesting comparison to be made with ideas such as that contained in Minsky's (1987) "society of mind." The socially embedded feature of polimorphic actions is *not reduced* by analysis into mimeomorphic elements. Higher-level polimorphic actions can be executed only by properly socially embedded actors. Entities that reproduce the behaviors corresponding to the lowest level of an action tree would not be able to match the choice of behaviors to social context that is required if a polimorphic action is to be successfully executed.

The reason nearly all actions terminate in mimeomorphic actions is that as we go down the tree structure, we reach ever more precisely specified action types, and almost inevitably we cease to care how these already highly specified actions are further specified. We cannot care about the exact way we carry out the most minute elements of our actions because humans' ability to attend to detail is not that great.

This is not to say that the bodily movements to which we never attend are found at a fixed level. There are bodily movements that we do not normally attend to, which are "things we do in order to do actions rather than being actions themselves"; but at different times and places even these might turn into actions. For example, though it is nearly always the case that when our heart is beating it is making it possible for us to do other actions rather than comprising an action itself, the invention of "biofeedback technology" carries with it new possibilities. Perhaps we could turn the working of the heart muscles into an action, narrowly conceived; this in turn carries with it the possibility of heartbeating becoming a formative action.

We have to say that *nearly* all actions terminate in mimeomorphic actions, because there seem to be cases where it would be petty to press the point. For example, the action of hand-writing a letter, rather than using a typewriter, is best thought of as terminating in a playful polimorphic action of the personalized variety; the inscriptions of the pen are the last thing we attend to, and we try to vary these. But playful mimeomorphic actions are, as we have explained, a hybrid category. Perhaps it is the case that all action trees terminate in actions in which the exact specification of the behavior is not meaningful—they terminate, then, either in mimeomorphic actions or in playful polimorphic actions. We will take this to be the case.

Putting together the last few paragraphs, we find that if we extend actions trees far enough they are always polimorphic at the top and (nearly) always mimeomorphic at the bottom. When we say an action is a polimorphic action, we know it will almost always have mimeomorphic actions embedded in it. Conversely, when we say an action is mimeomorphic, we know that it will be embedded in a polimorphic action.

4

A Theory of Interaction

So far we have examined types of intentional formative actions as they are executed by individuals.[1] But the overall purpose of this book is to understand the interaction between humans and humans, on the one hand, and between humans and machines, on the other. Our theory of interaction rests upon the distinctions and tree structures introduced in the last chapter.

The coordination of intentional actions implies that the actors understand the intentions of those they interact with. Put differently, coordination of actions presupposes a shared form of life. We shall deal with interaction within a culture in the first part of this chapter. In the second part we shall turn to forms of interactions that do not presuppose a common form of life. In our terminology, this comes down to the problem of coordinating action, not with other action, but with behavior. Using another's behavior for achieving one's goals does not presuppose that the other identify this behavior under the same, or indeed, under any intention as an action. To give a readily understood example, ruthless parents might use the all-night screaming of their infant in order to expel their neighbors, but the infant will not be able to identify its behavior as any part of its parents' plan. The infant is not yet a competent member of its parents' culture. The second part of the treatment will begin with an analysis of coordination across cultures.

1. This is not to deny of course that there is an important class of intentional formative actions that are executed by collectives and that cannot be reduced to actions executed by individuals—for instance the action of having an argument. As far as we can see, this distinction is orthogonal to our theory.

Action Coordination within a Culture

We will distinguish between *vertical* and *horizontal* coordination of actions/behaviors; where we have vertical coordination we will refer to action *cascades*, whereas horizontal coordinations will be referred to as *conjugations*. In an action cascade, one actor, say X, carries out an action for another actor, say Y, such that X's action is a subaction within the action of X. For instance, X might, upon Y's command, throw a switch and thereby turn on the light for Y. In this case, it seems natural to say that Y turned on the light by ordering X to throw the appropriate switch. We call this a vertical action coordination, or action cascade, because X's action is situated on a branch of Y's action tree.

In the case of action conjugations, the actions of those who interact are not instances of one actor's carrying out a subaction of the other's action; instead the achievement of each actor's goals makes it useful, pleasurable, or even imperative for them to coordinate their actions with one another. Think for example of two people having an argument: Here there is no hierarchical structure such that the one uses the other in order to achieve his or her goal (except in the broad and vague sense that each of the two needs the other to argue).[2]

Subcategories of action cascades and action conjugations can be defined by using the action theory developed in the last chapter. We can distinguish between cases where the set of coordinated actions consists solely of polimorphic actions, where it consists only of mimeomorphic actions, and where it consists of both polimorphic and mimeomorphic actions. As we shall see, looking at action coordination in this way will allow us to redescribe some familiar models of social organization within our theoretical framework.

Action Cascades

Recall that in our action trees, higher nodes stand for types of actions that are realized (in part) by more precisely defined action types lower down the tree. Thus "turning on the light yourself and with your left

2. As can be seen, if we were to deal with the issue of irreducibly collective action, our theory of action conjugation would be our starting point.

hand" (= d) falls under "turning on the light yourself" (= b), which in turn falls under "turning on the light" (= a) (see figure 4.1). Now attend to the right-hand branch (below c) of figure 4.1. The dotted line is meant to capture the possibility that the actor who carries out the action of turning on the light might be able to do so, and choose to do so, by asking or commanding another actor to throw the switch. The first actor would still be the actor who carries out the action of turning on the light.

We indicate the shift from one actor to another actor by a dotted line drawn at the node where the shift occurs. Thus in figure 4.1 we draw the line at node c. The dotted line can be entered at any node according to the point at which the action is delegated. This then is *action delegation*.

Note that the dotted line is a little more than a way of dividing up an action tree into separate areas of responsibility. The dotted line must, as it were, "contain" an action comprising delegation, which would not be there if the same individual were responsible for the action all the way down. The action of delegation might terminate in the uttering of some words, the waving of a flag, the pressing of a button, the raising of an eyebrow, or some such. This behavior is what terminates the upper section of the action tree and turns it into something that can be construed as a completely realized action in itself.

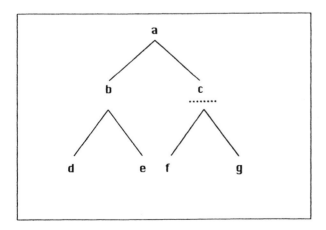

Figure 4.1
Turning on the light.

Given that there are two types of actions, polimorphic and mimeo-morphic, to be arranged in a vertical hierarchy, four arrangements are possible:

1. *Polimorphic action cascades:* action cascades where immediately both above and below the dotted line we find polimorphic actions.
2. *Mimeomorphic action cascades:* action cascades where immediately both above and below the dotted line we find mimeomorphic actions.
3. *Control cascades:* action cascades where immediately above the line we have a polimorphic action, and immediately below the line mimeo-morphic actions.
4. *Indifference cascades:* action cascades where immediately above the line we have a mimeomorphic action, and immediately below the line polimorphic actions.

Figure 4.2 summarizes these distinctions in diagrammatic form. Instances of each of the four logically possible cases of action cascade are readily found in social life.

Polimorphic Action Cascades

Organizations that produce "crafted" goods through the hierarchical cooperation of employers/managers and workers involve higher level polimorphic actions in a cascade with lower level polimorphic actions. The painting workshops of the Renaissance were like this; a master painter such as Michaelangelo would sketch out the main outlines of the picture and, perhaps, the faces, leaving it to apprentices or specialists to paint in clothes, curtains, and other more straightforward features. Every aspect of the painting, from top to bottom of the action cascade, turned on the skilled execution of polimorphic actions, set in a sea of social convention, yet all of these actions contributed toward the execution of the Michelangelo's overall action, "painting."

Woodworking workshops would have been similar. Apprentices may have been asked to turn out chair legs, or wheel spokes, or banister rails, each item requiring the apprentice to understand how to cut a piece of wood into pieces with a view to maximizing strength and productivity in the context of the grain, the knots in the wood, and the social acceptability of a chair leg or banister rail with a certain appearance. As with the painting of pictures, the apprentices would need to understand

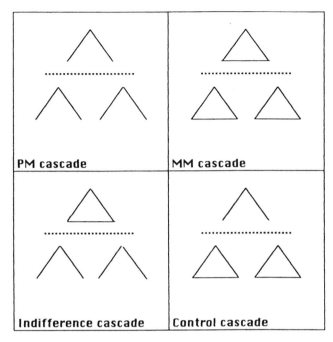

Figure 4.2
Different types of action cascade.

the overall aim of the exercise much as the master understood it, or they would not be able to fulfill their role. Nevertheless, the master was the organizer—the instigator of the action cascade in which the apprentices were embedded.

Mimeomorphic Action Cascades
As we will argue more fully in chapter 8, cascades of mimeomorphic actions are found in armies. For example, on a parade ground a sergeant major will give orders to the troops in such a stylized manner that the sounds are almost unrecognizable as words belonging to a natural language. The sergeant major is engaging in mimeomorphic actions—turning himself into a machine—as a theatrical symbol of the machinelike performance that is demanded of the troops. The troops respond with actions that are equally mimeomorphic.

Control Cascades

The most obvious example of a control cascade is a Taylorist production line. Managers execute control, changing shift patterns and so forth, in response to shifting social and industrial environments, but the workers they control are meant to carry out mimeomorphic actions only.

In an army, a control cascade is found between the levels of command who are expected to control the battle responsively, and those who are expected to control the firing in the line. Above that transition point are found polimorphic action cascades, below it are found mimeomorphic action cascades; the transition point is a control cascade. It may be hard to find this ideal in the modern army, but it seems probably that it did work out like this in the days of musket volleys (see chapter 8).

Indifference Cascades

Indifference cascades are the fruit of certain modern management systems. According to Agre (1994), this kind of cascade is encouraged by the development of computer systems that can log the activity of workers ever more intrusively. He gives the example of the management of a restaurant. Waiters are issued with magnetic cards and must "swipe" their card through a reader whenever they complete the serving of a meal. Their pay is determined by the number of swipes/servings they complete.

In this system the "management" need do no more than respond with predetermined outputs of money in response to inputs of swipes. The waiters, however, must serve the food in a way that responds to circumstance. They must understand what the customers want, they must serve with a smile if they are to avoid customer complaints, they must cope with children, with disabled customers, with drunk customers, with the full range of meals that a customer might order, with orders that the restaurant may be unable to fill—sometimes even when the item is on the menu—and they must cope with complaints, returns of food, and so forth. Thus, although the managers' task (of counting meals) can be completed through mimeomorphic actions alone, the waiters must engage in polimorphic actions.

One further aspect of indifference cascades is worth noting. Recall that in the last chapter we pointed out that a tree structure in which we have open triangles immediately below a closed triangle is impossible (figure 3.10). Now we can see that this claim holds only for the action tree of a single agent. Once we remove this restriction, that is, once we allow for a shift of agency within an action tree (dashed lines at nodes of a tree structure), it is no longer impossible.

Extended Cascades

Above we have focused on action cascades with just two layers, or one dotted line. Nothing in our theory hinders us from extending cascades to more than two layers. Obviously, such iterated action delegation can take many different forms. For example, in military chains of command the orders flow downward from politicians, to high-ranking officers, through signalers, through lower-ranking officers, through noncommissioned officers, to the private soldiers. Here we find polimorphic actions ordering mimeomorphic actions (of the signalers), ordering polimorphic actions (of the lower ranking officers and "noncoms"), ordering mimeomorphic actions (the soldiers).

Changing Cascades

The character of interaction cascades sometimes changes as the organization changes. Strangely enough, favored models of effective management seem to have moved from a polimorphic action cascade model—suited to craft enterprises—through a period involving indifference cascades (managers giving well-defined orders to skilled workers), control cascades (creative entrepreneurs designing behaviorally specific tasks—as in Taylorism), and mimeomorphic action cascades (where lower-order managers are given completely defined tasks to execute and have them carried out by workers whose behavior is fully controlled), back to a polimorphic action cascade model—managers wanting teamwork and commitment from their employees so as to cope with the demands of a rapidly changing technological environment.[3] In this, the

3. See Walton (1985) and Sundstrom, DeMeuse, and Futrell (1990). The change from indifference cascade to control and mimeomorphic action cascades is also central to Foucault's history of modalities of power. Foucault is interested in the disciplining, controlling, and manipulating of human bodies. Examples he gives of the power mechanisms invented and used in the seventeenth and eighteenth centuries include both mechanisms that depend on coercer and coerced sharing the same form of life, and mechanisms that do not. Among the latter can be

movement has been similar to that involved in the longer march of military history from privateering, through the musket and trench warfare, to modern mobile war involving independent units coordinated by radio.[4]

Delegation and Moral Responsibility Are Orthogonal

For some types of action cascades, those involved in the lower levels need to understand the purposes of the cascade as a whole, while for others they do not. For instance, in the case of Taylorism, where the production-line worker is given a "behavioral plan" to follow, there is no need for those executing the lower reaches of the tree to understand the overall purpose. (Whether this is an efficient method of organization is not our concern.) In the case of all four types of cascade, examples can be found in which the lower-level actors either do or do not understand the overall picture. For example, the members of a synchronized swimming team are the final element in a control cascade; they do understand the overall purpose of what they are doing. "Native dancers" might also be the final element in the control cascade of an entrepreneur who uses them in a money-earning spectacle; the entrepreneur's plan would work just as well if the dancers did not know that they were dancing to make money. Cricketers and soccer players are components in polimorphic action cascades; they are quite aware of their contributions to the overall performance of the team. Spies or the members of an elite army squad are also contributors to polimorphic action cascades, but they may be given objectives that fit into an overall plan in ways they cannot imagine. The plot of *The Spy Who Came in from the Cold* exemplifies this point. Commando raids designed to inflict enough damage to bolster morale on the "home front" without seriously affecting the enemy's ability to wage war may be executed by soldiers who do not understand the narrowly conceived ineffectiveness of their sacrifice.

---

counted spatial-architectural arrangements that constrain people's movements. Foucault sees no distinction between the two cases in the way that we do. See, for example, Foucault (1977), Kusch (1991).

4. See De Landa (1991). This book does not say much of interest about war in the age of intelligent machines, but does include a fascinating history of military organization. We discuss the military further in a later chapter.

Though the actors at the bottom of the cascade do not need to understand the whole of the action to which they contribute, in the case of polimorphic action cascades they do need to share a form of life with those at the top. The actors at the top will have no hope of carrying out their actions unless they are able to foresee what the actors at the bottom will do in various circumstances; that is, they have to know that their instructions will be carried out, and roughly how their instructions will be carried out. The actors at the bottom have to understand the instructions; they have to know what their leaders appear to want them to do, though their leaders may not always be frank about the purpose they have in mind. But even deception involves sharing a form of life.[5]

Let us consider the matter using the language of results and consequences discussed in chapter 2. In *The Spy Who Came in from the Cold*, Leamas's intention is to have Mundt arrested. Having Mundt arrested is the result of the action he intended. But the result of the action Smiley intended is to have Fiedler arrested, and this turns out to be the consequence of Leamas's action only if what Leamas did *fails* to have the result he intended. In the case of the commando group, the soldiers' intention is, say, to inflict damage on an enemy installation (possibly at great cost to themselves). The intention of the politicians who control them is to bolster morale on the home front. Bolstering morale will be a consequence of the commando group carrying out their actions and *achieving* the results they intend—inflicting damage on the enemy installation. It may be important to the politicians, however, to leave the commandos in ignorance of their (the politicians') intentions. The intention of bolstering morale may not motivate the commandos to sacrifice themselves. Therefore the politicians will want to convince the commandos that they are attacking a target that is important from a more narrow point of view (e.g., they will lead the commandos to believe that success will deprive the enemy of important resources that could otherwise be used to kill many more of their comrades).

In the case of the spy, the spymaster is interested in the failure of the spy's mission, though it is vital that the spy does not know this and that the spy does his best to succeed; in the case of the commandos, both

5. See Collins (1983).

politicians and commandos are interested in the success of the commando mission, even though success figures in different ways in their respective intentions. It seems that the relationship between delegation of actions and certain moral categories are complex and often orthogonal.[6]

Still more important from the point of view of the overall theory, all parties in both cases have to share an understanding of the actions in which they are involved. Therefore they have to share a culture and a form of life, and agree about the intended results of the *delegatee's* actions. What they do not have to share is knowledge of the intended results of the *delegators'* actions; that is, they do not have to share knowledge of the planned consequences of the delegated actions.

Action Conjugations

Above, we distinguished vertical from horizontal action coordination. We call horizontal action coordination *action conjugation*. As before, we can identify subcategories. With action cascades there were four logical possibilities, identified by combining our two basic types of action in a hierarchy. In action conjugations the hierarchical differentiation is lost, so that what were two distinct kinds of *mixed action cascade* collapse into one type of *mixed action conjugation*, giving three types of conjugation in all, each with counterparts in real life:

1. In *polimorphic action conjugations,* both actors engage in polimorphic actions. For instance, during most everyday conversations, we vary our linguistic behavior in response to the interlocutor's utterances, as well as to changes in the environment. Some linguistic behavior consists of *open polimorphic actions,* some consists of *occasioned polimorphic actions,* and some consists of *playful polimorphic actions.*

2. In *mimeomorphic action conjugations,* both actors are engaged in mimeomorphic actions. For instance, in the U.S. military, a system has been used to make sure that no soldier can, on his own, launch a nuclear missile; to open the missile silo, two soldiers, at some distance from one another, have to turn two different keys simultaneously. Other examples can be found in team sports, such as synchronized swimming, or in the

---

6. It is also worth noting that this argument has no bearing whatsoever on the so-called Nuremberg defense—that an actor carries no culpability if he or she is "only following orders." Following orders can be done with or without awareness of the meaning and consequences of the action and therefore with or without culpability.

"Mexican wave," or, of course, in military exercises. Choreographed dances, such as those in Busby Berkeley musicals, or the shows put on during mass gatherings where each member of a vast crowd hold up a colored card that together form the features of the face of Mao, or some such, are yet further examples. (These latter examples also have the features of an action cascade, if one takes the choreographer into account.)

3. In *mixed action conjugations*, one of the actors executes polimorphic actions, while the other executes mimeomorphic actions. Think, for instance, of certain military training regimes in which new recruits are forced to respond to all utterances by their superiors with a single phrase such as "yes sir." Or think of a soccer team defending the goal against a free kick; the players forming the "wall" do mimeomorphic actions—they stand still, while the goalkeeper does polimorphic action.

These cases are represented by drawing the two tree structures side by side, separating them with a vertical dashed line, as in figure 4.3.

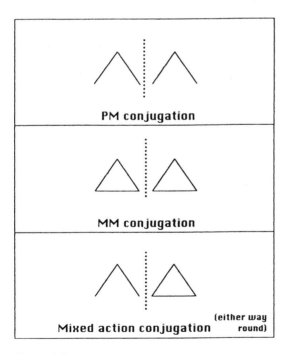

PM conjugation

MM conjugation

Mixed action conjugation   (either way round)

Figure 4.3
Action conjugations.

Coordination across Cultures: The "Behaver Tribe"

We now turn to the coordination of actions where there is no shared form of life, that is, the coordination of action with the behavioral counterpart of action. We are interested in this phenomenon since the coordination of actions across forms of life helps us to understand at least some aspects of the delegation of our actions to what we will call "behavers"—nonhumans such as animals or machines.

Action and behavior may be combined vertically, in a hierarchy, or horizontally. Real life exhibits each of the seven logically possible combinations of actions *within* a culture. Are there equivalent real-life examples where actions are coordinated *across* cultures? The answer is "no"; there are some empty boxes.

In our diagrams, the coordination of the actions of one actor with the behaviors corresponding to the actions of an actor belonging to another culture are represented by solid lines instead of by the dashed lines we used to indicate coordination within cultures. As with the dashed lines, the solid lines "contain" something that mediates the switching of responsibility from one entity to another. The solid line may contain a "signal," or it may contain an act of delegation. Where the act of delegation results in the control of someone's or something's behavior by "higher-level" polimorphic actions, the solid line will have to include an act of "digitization" of the polimorphic action so that there are signals that can be acted upon by an entity that does not understand the polimorphic action.

Figure 4.4 shows the three possible types of action-behavior coordination across cultures. To exemplify the difference between coordination within and across cultures, consider a rowing team. All members have an interest in rowing smoothly so as to maximize the speed of their craft through the water. They follow the directions of the "cox," who coordinates their actions, to help each member achieve his or her individual goal of making his or her own stroke mimeomorphic. The rowers and the cox share a form of life and an aim in life. But now think of a Roman galley powered by slaves who know not where their boat is going nor why. Led by the sound of the drum beat, the slaves know only that they must row hard and with as much coordination as possible. The boat

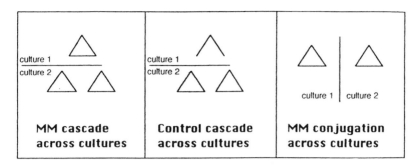

Figure 4.4
Coordination across cultures.

moves smoothly and rapidly through the water. The rowers and the slave masters still share a form of life, though they have different interests in the consequences of their actions.

Now imagine that the slaves who understand the concept of rowing are replaced by slaves who do not even know that they are on a boat. They are trained under a "behaviorist" regime to pull on poles with a certain movement and rhythm—success brings food while failure brings pain. Imagine that those slaves develop their own credo. They believe, say, that they have been captured by the angry God of Storms who is using them to propel thunder clouds (the drumming) across the heavens. If they do the god honor by rowing hard, their good performance will lead not only to their own salvation but also to the salvation of their ancestors and offspring. Again, the boat moves smoothly through the water, though initial training may have taken some time. Now there are two forms of life providing the context for the actions of masters and slaves respectively; there is no sharing of a conceptual world. What is shared is behavior alone. In such a case, the drumming is the means by which the galley master's warlike actions are digitized so that they can be delegated to the slaves.

Now imagine that the ignorant slaves are replaced with trained apes. And now imagine that the trained apes are replaced with machinery. We are concerned with the conditions under which series of replacements of this kind would allow the delegators' actions to have the intended effects (in this case, the boat is rowed).

Consider again the case where the galley master is using the behaviors corresponding to the slaves' religious actions to carry out the rowing he wants done. Not any old religiously motivated behavior will do. Somehow the slaves have had to come to the conclusion that the proper way to serve the God of Storms is via mimeomorphic actions and mimeomorphic actions alone—coordinated pole pulling. Were religious observance among these slaves to be served from time to time by still and silent meditation, they would not make a useful galley crew. The general point is this: Where behaviors corresponding to another culture's *actions* are to be incorporated into an action cascade or conjugation, it is necessary (though not sufficient) that the other culture's actions be mimeomorphic. If they are not, the behaviors of the others will not be predictable enough to be used; for example, in this case the behaviors of the slaves will be ordered according to a context that the galley master does not understand. But if the actions are mimeomorphic, the galley master does not have to understand the context to grasp the order in the behaviors. That another culture engages in mimeomorphic actions does not mean that we can always incorporate their actions, but it creates the possibility.

We know, of course, that these are artificial examples. Real-life exploitation is done differently, by making cultures homogeneous. Pop music, McDonalds, and Western-style schools and universities homogenize culture in one direction, and various influences come back the other way. But cultural homogenization, or "globalization," solves no theoretical problems. We need to think of, possibly, artificial examples in which the two cultures that interest us are hermetically sealed. This is because we are trying to understand how we exploit a "tribe" that is completely sealed off from us culturally—the tribe of things, or the "behaver tribe." For the members of this tribe, globalization of culture will work only if we allow *them* all the privileges of the imperialist and adapt ourselves to their ways; we cannot socialize them with pop music or branches of McDonald's—they just won't be socialized.

Cross-cultural and Human-Machine Coordination
Let us now work through the seven types of action-action coordination and ask in each case whether there is any element that can be replaced by behavior alone. Figure 4.5 summarizes the distinctions made so far

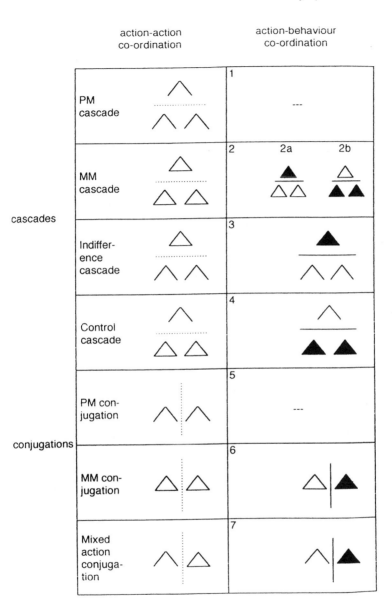

Figure 4.5
Working with behavers.

and sets out the conclusions we are about to reach. We adopt one final diagrammatic convention: Behaviors alone are not actions. Behavior, even when it mimics the behavior associated with a mimeomorphic action, will be represented by a solid rather than an empty triangle.

Starting at the top of the figure, no element of a polimorphic action cascade can be replaced by behavior alone, and therefore no element can be replaced by the actions of members of another culture. This is because the behavior corresponding to a polimorphic action has to be responsive to social circumstances and the recognition of, and response to, circumstances requiring familiarity with the relevant form of life. For the same reason, no element of a polimorphic action conjugation can be replaced by behavior alone. Thus boxes 1 and 5 are empty.

Working down the figure, either element of a mimeomorphic action cascade can be replaced by behavior alone. In the earlier section we used military drill, led by a sergeant major, as our example—or a mimeomorphic action cascade. We can imagine the sergeant major being replaced by a tape recorder carrying prerecorded cries of command designed to be transmitted at exactly the right intervals. A sergeant major with a sore throat might decide to use such a device for training his troops (box 2a).[7] If the sergeant major could be replaced by an entity with as little relevant socialization as a tape recorder, we can imagine him or her being replaced by a person from an unfamiliar culture whose mimeomorphic actions designed for some other end happen to involve the utterance of a series of sergeant major–like screams at the relevant intervals. (Actually, it is almost impossible to imagine this, but the point of principle stands.) We can also imagine a short story in which a mynah bird comes to imitate a sergeant major and comes to control the troops either by accident or as a sadistic game.

We can also just about imagine the troops being replaced by members of another culture. These might already like to march for some reason or another and the only element of training required would be to make

---

7. Just as it is incorrect to talk of a machine "acting," it is equally incorrect to talk of a machine "delegating" or "ordering." We can, however, talk of the machine mimicking mimeomorphic versions of the actions of delegating or ordering.

their marching correspond to the relevant shouts and screams. More reasonably, we can imagine people who did not share a culture being trained to march without really acting at all. Indeed, the very aim of initial military training could be said to strip the recruits of their socialization—to make them respond without considering, even for a fraction of a second, the purpose of their movements, the possibility of disobeying an order, or the possibility of adjusting the way an order is executed according to social circumstances (chapter 8 considers this example further).[8] It is harder to imagine marching done by literal machines, but that is because we cannot imagine what the purpose would be, not because we cannot imagine the proper movements being carried out.[9]

In the same way, we can imagine either element of a mimeomorphic action conjugation being replaced by "behavers" (box 6). In the case of the two soldiers who must turn the keys to the nuclear warhead simultaneously, we can imagine a mad soldier training a monkey to turn the second key so as to circumvent the safeguard; the very point would be that the monkey did not understand that turning the key would lead to mass destruction. We can also imagine machines or animals taking the place of various members of the choreographed teams we discussed under this heading.

We have now discussed four out the seven possibilities, leaving just the three that involve mixtures of mimeomorphic actions and polimorphic actions. The pattern of argument is probably predictable by now. Each mimeomorphic action element of the cascade or conjugation can be replaced by behavior, whether it be that pertaining to a mimeomorphic action defined by a different intention in the foreign tribe, by a set of bodily movements trained by "behaviorist" methods (either in a human or an animal), or by behaviors carried out by a machine. Let us see if this idea works for the remaining three cases.

Our example of an "indifference cascade," in which a polimorphic action falls below a mimeomorphic action in the action tree, was the

8. This, let it be stressed, is a poor way to run a modern army in a well-educated society.
9. See Collins (1990) for a discussion of marching carried out by "machine-assisted" troops.

management system in a modern restaurant using "swipe cards" to control the waiting staff. In this system it is the manager who is easily replaced, whereas the waiters are not (unless the restaurant changes its character). There seems no reason why the manager (at least insofar as the manager's role concerns supervising pay rewards) should not be replaced by a machine (box 3). (The whole idea of the time clock was perhaps an early instance of such a trend.)

Our examples of control cascades, in which mimeomorphic actions fall below polimorphic actions, were Taylorism and the relevant level of the military. Taylorism was, of course, a step toward full automation of the production line, though since Taylorism hardly ever worked properly, the next steps were far harder than anyone imagined. As far as the military is concerned, the same applies; the ideal musketeer would have no concept of the purpose and possible consequences of his actions, but would merely follow orders like an automaton. (As we have said, if the actions below the solid line are to be genuinely mimeomorphic, the solid line must contain something that digitizes the polimorphic actions above it into appropriate "signals.") Neither the Taylorist manager nor the commander of the muskets could be replaced by animals or machines, however (box 4).

Finally, our examples of action conjugations involving both polimorphic actions and mimeomorphic actions were early military training and a soccer team defending against a free kick. A mynah bird could fulfill the role of the recruit, shouting "yes sir" to every utterance (though it would be a purposeless replacement since the whole point of the exercise is to train a human). A wall of bricks of the same size could replace the defensive "wall" of players but could not replace the goalkeeper.

The Argument Revisited

The first part of this chapter sets out and exemplifies various types of action coordination under circumstances in which all the actors share a form of life. That is to say, the first part examines the ways in which parts of action trees can be delegated to, or otherwise carried out by, other actors who share an understanding of the actions essayed.

The second part of the chapter explores the circumstances under which the constraint of a shared form of life can be relaxed. It is found that all mimeomorphic action elements in cascades and conjugations can be carried out by those who live in radically discontinuous cultures. This, we admitted, was rarely a realistic scenario, especially in a time of increasing cultural homogeneity; nevertheless, the idea of radical cultural discontinuity serves a useful analytic purpose.

Those who do not share a culture can be led to carry out the relevant behavior in a variety of ways. One way is to take some existing mimeomorphic actions in the radically unfamiliar culture and incorporate the behaviors associated with them into one's action trees. Special (and perhaps bizarre) circumstances will be needed before such a strategy can succeed, and it may have been done rarely, if ever. To search for real-life examples, one would go back into the annals of enslavement and look for those forced to work treadmills or the like.

On the other hand, one might look into recent analyses of science which are related to Thomas Kuhn's idea of paradigm revolution. The idea of radical cultural discontinuity has resurfaced in studies of science. Thus a scientific measurement may indicate one thing within one paradigm and something else within a different paradigm. Using measurements made for a different purpose in this way is, effectively, taking over a set of behaviors, and incorporating them in a set of actions for which they were never intended (Collins and Pinch 1982).

In incorporating the actions of those belonging to a radically unfamiliar culture, one is really interested only in their behaviors. Once one sees this, it is a short step to seeing that a set of behaviors may be evinced by training methods that require no socialization at all, and therefore they may be exhibited by entities that are not social in the sense of being "members of a form of life." Such entities include humans who are treated as animals, animals themselves, and computers and the like.[10]

10. This is what is going on in the attempts to model scientific discovery with computers (Collins 1989); it is not discovery that is being modeled, but a certain kind of asocial discovery behavior.

5

Morphicity and Human Competence

Situated Action Paths and Action Channels

To show how the analysis of action morphicity helps us understand how humans gain competence, we must first describe routes through action trees.[1] The recent literature on action theory suggests that an intention to act is best understood as some kind of rational commitment (Bratman 1987; Moya 1990). To form the intention today to travel to London tomorrow commits us to act in certain ways (e.g., not to buy a plane ticket to Toronto for tomorrow, not to arrange for meetings in Bath for tomorrow, and so forth). Of course such commitments can be overruled, but we would need a good reason. In addition to such "prior intentions"—that is, intentions to carry out actions at a later point in time—actors have "intentions-in-action"—that is, the intention to do what they are doing when they are doing it (Searle 1983). These intentions-in-action need not be explicitly formulated, but as we remarked in an earlier chapter, they could be stated by at least some agents if we interrupted them and asked them what they were doing.

Action trees represent sets of possible ways of carrying out a higher-level action. Faced with such an action tree, an actor must take a route through it. Carrying out a polimorphic action often involves a sequence of situated choices; after the initial commitment to the action, the agent still needs to fix, creatively, a number of parameters of the action.

1. There are some large contributions to this chapter from previously published sources. We are particularly grateful to Gerard de Vries and Wiebe Bijker for allowing us to use ideas originally published in Collins, de Vries, and Bijker (1997).

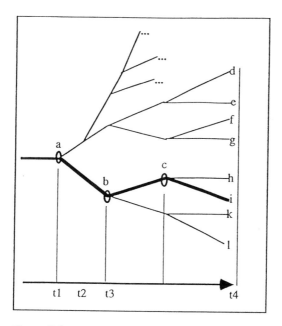

Figure 5.1
Path through an action tree.

Rotating our action trees into the conventional sideways position, we can represent this situation as follows. After the actor has formed the intention to carry out action "a," he or she still needs to make further decisions and thus needs to form further choices or "subintentions" that settle the details of the action path represented by the heavy line in figure 5.1.[2]

The term "choices" describes the route through a polimorphic action tree, but matters are subtly different in the case of mimeomorphic actions. If "a" were a *singular mimeomorphic action,* there would be no *choices* in the normal sense to be made at nodes "b" or "c"—at least, not if the action was to be executed successfully. Either there is a plan already in

2. As we explain in a later chapter, our discussion of the matter in terms of "sequence," "before," "after," and so forth can give a misleading impression of orderly temporal flow; the order is essentially logical. Sometimes all the choices will be made at once and sometimes the causal ordering of choices will run both up and down the action tree.

place that determines the route so that the whole tree could be said to collapse into a single route, or, looked at another way, and taking into account that all mimeomorphic actions have width if looked at from the appropriate frame of reference, the route through "b," "c," and so forth, is a matter of *indifference*, not choice.

If the tree represented a sequence of disjunctive mimeomorphic actions, the matter would be subtly different again. In that case the route taken at each node would not be a matter of indifference, but it would be determined in one way or another according to the circumstances pertaining at the node. To start with an easy example, if the mimeomorphic action were Taylorist chair spraying, the route would be determined by which shape of chair was passing down the production line as the actor passed across the relevant node. Thus, though the sequence of behaviors that would instantiate the actions at lower nodes may not be predictable in advance by any person, it would still not be a matter of actors' choices.

Routes through polimorphic action trees are, as we have said, determined by choices that refer to context; we will call these *situated action paths*. In contrast, routes through mimeomorphic action trees are much more like plans because they could, in principle, be specified fully without understanding the social context within which the action is set. But, since this kind of plan is not always made in advance, and since it may be beyond the capacity of humans to follow such plans even if they could be constructed, we will refer to these routes as *action channels*. Where action trees are mixed, as they usually are in real life, then the path has different characteristics at different places.

Human Competence and Machine Mimicry

Figure 5.2 shows examples of actions and their properties. We will work through each case in turn.[3] We want not simply to describe a list of competences, but to show how the idea of action morphicity helps us understand how these competences are learned, and to show that the

3. The rest of this chapter draws heavily on Collins, de Vries, and Bijker (1997), and Collins (1993).

	morph-icity 1	can be formul-ated 2	route through tree 3	how competence gained 4	level of awareness 5	skill-ful 6	can be mechan-ized 7	how mechan-ized 8
1a semaphor 1b pheasant plucker	mimeo	yes	plan	calculation	conscious	no yes	yes	program
2a marching 2b synchro-swimming	mimeo	yes	plan or channel	drill	conscious → internalised	no yes	yes	program
3 chair-spraying	mimeo	yes	channel	social skill practice	tacit	maybe	yes	research or record and playback
4 bike-balancing in the wild	mimeo	yes or potentially	channel	social skill practice	tacit	yes	yes	research or engineering
5 canoeing down rapids	mimeo	no because too complex	channel	social skill practice	tacit	yes	maybe	engineering
6 bike-riding in ordinary traffic	poli	no because socially embedded	situated action path	social skill	tacit	yes	yes	--------------
7 natural speech	poli	no because socially embedded	situated action path	social skill	tacit	no	no	--------------

Figure 5.2
Some actions and their properties.

polimorphic–mimeomorphic boundary does not correspond to other ways of dividing up our abilities.

Semaphor
In an earlier chapter we described how the word "Y-O-U" was made in semaphor. If we move along row 1a of figure 5.2, we find the properties of the action of semaphoring YOU in the various columns. Semaphoring YOU is a mimeomorphic action. The next column reminds us that a description of the action of semaphor signaling can be set down in a formula or code. The next column suggests that the route through the "semaphor YOU" action tree could be accomplished by advanced planning. Column 4 contains the claim that the kind of competence required

to semaphor YOU is that required to carry out a "calculation"; for most humans there is no need to practice or drill in order to accomplish the transformation of the code into the appropriate behavior, even if they have never before encountered semaphor. Column 5 suggests that semaphoring YOU—especially if one was a beginner—would be done consciously: It could be done reasonably efficiently without "internalizing" the routine. Column 6 suggests that semaphoring YOU is *not* what we normally think of as a skillful activity. The next column is a reminder that semaphoring could be mechanized, and the next that a suitable means of mechanization would be a computer program or similar device. For example, we can imagine a mechanical semaphor signaler arranged so that the arms moved to the positions corresponding to key presses on a computer keyboard, and that this would be managed by writing a suitable program with appropriate mechanical outputs to mechanical linkages.

Case 1b: Consider the test for alcoholic intoxication that, it was said, was used by the British police before the invention of the "breathalyzer." One was asked to articulate the phrase, "The Leith police dismisseth us." Now try repeating the following at high speed and without error:

I'm not a pheasant plucker
I'm a pheasant plucker's son,
And I'm only plucking pheasant
Till the pheasant pluckers come

Both the intoxication test and the recitation of the rhyme are like semaphor in that they are mimeomorphic actions which, to be carried out successfully, require an organized, specifiable set of movements—in this case of the vocal apparatus. These tasks can be done without difficulty by existing and conceivable talking computers. The difference between these tasks and semaphor is that they are thought of as skillful performances (when carried out by drunk and sober humans respectively). Presumably this has to do with the level of self-conscious deliberation needed to accomplish them. Attempts to say "the Leith police dismisseth us" while drunk are likely to fail if uttered without thought. Likewise, said without care, the rhyme tends to have disastrous results. Here we see that mimeomorphic actions can be called skilled or unskilled and, furthermore, that there is no need for a skill to be internalized to count as a skill.

Marching

Case 2a is marching (across a parade ground). This is mimeomorphic action and its associated behaviors can be formulated (as in, say, a diagram for the position of the feet). The movements associated with marching might be planned (imagine the parade ground painted with footsteps so as to indicate the position of soldiers' feet as a stage is marked with the position of actors' feet), or it might be that one step follows from another without preplanning the whole sequence; in the later case, the route through the action tree would be an action channel because the choices at each node in the action tree would not be socially situated, they would be forced by the logic of the march. Moving to columns 4 and 5, marching is usually mastered as a result of drill; novice marchers find it hard to accomplish the action with sufficient regularity and, while initial attempts at marching would be done self-consciously, the sequence of movement associated with good marching are better done by humans when they do *not* attend to them—that is, when the sequence has been internalized. Notice, however, that we do not refer to this internalized ability as "tacit knowledge" because it is quite evident that it has come from something that could be expressed in a formula, and it could be reexpressed in a formula should we so wish. Furthermore, we do not generally say of the action of marching across a parade ground that it is a skillful activity. Moving to columns 7 and 8, should we ever want to build a marching machine there would be no special difficulty in doing it; it would involve the same sort of programming and mechanical linkages as were discussed under the topic of semaphor.

It might be possible to pick holes in many of these claims about the properties of marching, but we need to say only that there is a variant of marching (or perhaps some other activity), that fits the profile we have laid out.

Synchronized swimming (2b) contrasts with marching in the same way as the "pheasant plucker" vocalization contrasts with semaphor. In this case, *both* marching and synchronized swimming are better performed when the rules are internalized, but the swimming is an Olympic-level skill, whereas marching is not generally referred to as demonstrating high levels of skill. What we think of as skillful or not skillful does not correspond to the polimorphic–mimeomorphic boundary, nor does self-conscious versus internalized performance.

Chair Spraying

What we have in mind in case 3 is the sort of chair spraying that takes place in a closed and controlled environment (e.g., Collins 1990). Chairs are transported along an assembly line, needing to be sprayed. A human holds a spray head, directing paint onto the bare surfaces of the chair until all is covered to an appropriate depth. A limited set of different kinds of chairs may be encountered, each requiring its own set of movements.

Chair spraying is a casual mimeomorphic action, and given the possibility of different shapes of chair arriving in front of the sprayer, it is a *casual disjunctive mimeomorphic action.* There is no question that the movements of the spray head required to coat the chair could be described using some kind of formal notation, but since a human chair sprayer does not and probably could not follow such a notation in order to carry out the actions, we would have to say that the route through the chair-spraying action tree is an *action channel.* Chair spraying is learned during a kind of apprenticeship—that is, the sprayer will be shown how to do the job and will master it with a little practice, rather than do it by a calculative process. The set of movements needed to spray a chair could not be written down in such a way that they could be followed by another person who had no understanding of what the job entailed. Given this, we would probably be inclined to say that the chair sprayer had gained some tacit knowledge, though nothing turns on whether this is the correct description in this particular case. We might be inclined to call a chair sprayer a skilled person, though the task is so quickly mastered that we might not.

Notice that though another person could not master chair spraying from a set of instructions unless he understood the point of the job—which is why we say the chair sprayer has tacit knowledge—there is no question but that the job could be mechanized. It could be mechanized by analyzing the movements necessary to coat a chair, and programming a device to reproduce those movements. Or it could be done by watching a human paint sprayer very closely, redescribing his or her behaviors in terms of space–time coordinates, and proceeding with the programming as before. Or it could be done, as it is usually done, by "record and playback"; in this case the movements of the spray head are transformed, and transmitted to magnetic tape or some such, so that the whole thing can be played back without anyone having to go to the trouble of noting down the space–time coordinates.

If we accept that it is correct to describe the human paint sprayer as having tacit knowledge, then it is clear that the tacitness of knowledge is in itself no obstacle to mechanization. The next example—riding a bicycle—makes matters still more clear.

Bike Balancing

As we will see, to understand bicycle riding we need to analyze it not only in terms of a vertical action tree, but also "horizontally," because bicycle riding might mean at least two different things; these vary in terms of their meaning as actions and in terms of the extent to which they can be mechanized. In the past, when bicycle riding has been used to exemplify human skills, these aspects have been confounded.

Bicycle riding is the classic example of the use of "tacit knowledge" (Polanyi 1958). Nevertheless, so long as we stick to bike riding in a wild, traffic-free landscape (so that interactions with other humans and human conventions do not come into play), we can also agree that there is a set of mathematico-physical rules that correctly describe the dynamics of bike riding. Let us call bike riding in a wild, traffic-free landscape "bike balancing."[4]

---

4. This is not to say that even bike balancing makes no contact with convention. The bicycle came to look the way it does as a result of the interplay of all kinds of social forces and all kinds of disputes about what it means to ride a bike (Bijker, Hughes, and Pinch 1987). What is more, bike balancing is embedded in an action tree that, like all action trees, becomes more polimorphic the further up we go. Without the embedding in society it is almost certain that what counts as the correct way to manage a bike would not emerge. Thus a person who encountered

The set of rules for balancing a bike is either known, or potentially known, to engineers. Notwithstanding, it is clear that when we ride a bike we humans do *not* manage it by the self-conscious application of a set of mathematico-physical rules, even if we are riding across a flat surface in still conditions. We do not do it this way because we cannot judge or measure angles and speeds fast and accurately enough, nor do the sums, nor apply the results quickly enough to keep the bike upright. If we were working in .00001 of earth's gravitational field, so that things happened a hundred thousand times more slowly, or if we were a hundred thousand times quicker in our calculating than we are, we possibly could do it.[5]

Bike balancing is a relatively complicated *casual disjunctive mimeo-morphic action*. It is an action that involves feedback. To repeat, the behaviors and responses that we need to carry out to keep a bike balanced are understandable and describable in physical terms, but they are still well beyond human mastery through self-conscious calculation, or

---

a bicycle for the first time on a "desert island" would probably never learn to ride, for it would not occur to them that a spindly framework with two spidery wheels, surmounted by a leather blade on a stick, could be made to balance if ridden at speed. A few trials would confirm the judgment. The novice bicycle rider learns that it can be done, that it should be done, and learns how hard it is to learn, from advice and example within the embedding society (Pinch, Collins, and Carbone 1996). That there are other ways of managing a bicycle is also what makes bike balancing a formative action. That bike balancing is embedded in a polimorphic action tree does not, however, make it a polimorphic action.

Incidentally, nothing said here about the possibility of formulating a description of the physics of bike riding conflicts with ideas in the sociology of scientific knowledge. The formula may be a result of social agreements but we must still talk of a formula, for this is what a social agreement generates; there is nothing more correct than this.

5. For "Trekkies," Mr. Data is a good model. In one episode of *Star Trek* Commander Crusher shows Mr. Data the steps of a dance. She shows them only once. Mr. Data is immediately able to repeat them; Mr. Data has the kind of quick brain we are talking about. Unfortunately for *Star Trek*, Commander Crusher then tells Mr. Data to improvise, and he does this too. Improvisation is a skill requiring social embedding of a sort that Mr. Data seems to lack on other occasions. Social sensitivity is needed to know that one innovative dance step counts as an improvisation while another counts as foolishness. Thus *Star Trek* has not fully anticipated the arguments of this book.

through drill. Such skills are nearly always mastered through practice within a supporting and guiding social community.[6]

Can bike balancing be mechanized? It can, and it has. Gyrostar (1992) uses a gyroscope and attitude sensing. With something as complicated as bike balancing, mechanization is often achieved more easily through engineering solutions than through ever more ramified symbolic programming.

Canoeing Down Rapids

In one place, Suchman (1993) discusses the navigation of a canoe through a set of rapids as an example of what she calls a situated action (Suchman 1987).[7] In our terminology, we would say that canoeing down rapids is an extremely complicated *casual disjunctive mimeomorphic action*. Let us continue to be guided by the sequence of columns in figure 5.2. The action of canoeing down rapids is almost certainly too complicated to be expressed in formulaic terms, though the limitation here is one of physics; it is probably that the variations of magnitudes of forces in a fast-flowing stream are too great to foresee, and the way rocks and waves might be used to slide the canoe in different directions is equally a matter of fortuitous judgments. It is likely that the stream is impossible to model usefully, either mathematically or computationally, because of its complexity and perhaps even because there are chaotic effects rendering the links between cause and effect indeterminable, if not indeterminate. Continuing across the columns of figure 5.2, the route through the action tree of canoeing down a rapid is, in our language, an *action channel.* Canoeing is generally learned through apprenticeship with practice in a

---

6. As explained in previous chapters, the morphicity of actions may change over time. Bike balancing could become something else. Imagine a society in which it was thought to be bad form to ride in a state of balance all the time, and that the cute way to ride a bike was by doing "wheelies," falling off now and again, and generally "acting the clown" (see Bijker, Hughes, and Pinch 1987) for a discussion of the changing role of the bicycle). In that case, bike riding, even across a wild landscape, could not be accomplished by mimeomorphic actions because knowing the right way to ride would involve continual reference to one's audience.

7. The journal volume in which Suchman paper is found contains other examples of so-called situated actions that exhibit nothing more philosophically profound in the way of difficulty than physical complexity.

context of social support. The knowledge, once acquired, is tacit and there is no question that we refer to the ability as skillful.

Can canoeing be mechanized? It is hard to say until someone tries. No existing machine could replace the human in the canoe, but this may be just because no one has yet tried hard enough; after all, a mechanical canoeist is not something for which there is great demand. Nevertheless, from our point of view there is no principled objection to the possibility of a mechanized canoeist. Perhaps big neural nets or "situated robots" could do the job one day. Perhaps it is will be a matter of clever engineering. After all, a stick tossed in the water does quite well on its own. Not everything that cannot be mechanized cannot be mechanized because of polimorphicity; there is physical complexity too.

Bike Riding

Moving down the rows of figure 5.2, we come to a double horizontal line. Above this line all the actions are mimeomorphic, while the two below it are polimorphic. The first instance of a polimorphic action that we deal with is ordinary bicycle riding as opposed to bike balancing. Ordinary bike riding involves interaction with traffic, and traffic-controlling conventions such as traffic lights, road signs, junctions, curbs, verges, and so forth. This element of bike riding is a matter of polimorphic actions.

One might ask of a bicycle rider, "Why did you cross the junction in front of that car coming from your right?" He or she might reply: "I exchanged glances with the driver." But this does not provide a repertoire for junction crossing, since the context is so crucial. It depends on the country in which the bike is being ridden, along with an estimate of the moral integrity of its inhabitants and the particular car driver in question; it depends on whether the rider has a child on board; and, of course, it depends on the nature of the glances. Given what are otherwise the "same" circumstances, the wisdom of the move can change over time and place as the relative status of cars and bikes changes (Collins, de Vries, and Bijker 1997).

Adopting the columnar scheme once more and going to column 2, the behaviors required for ordinary bike riding cannot be formulated. Unlike the case of canoeing down rapids, however, the case is not one of the complexity of the physics, but of the social embedding of the action. The route through the action is a matter of making situated choices at nodes, so it can be neither a plan nor a channel; it is a *situated action path*. The way bike riding is mastered is undoubtedly as a social skill, and the knowledge is tacit. It is what we refer to as a skillful activity. Crucially, it cannot be mechanized unless the mechanism can be embedded somehow into the flux of social life in the same way as a bike rider is embedded. Therefore the box in the last row is blank.

Natural Speech

Ordinary language speaking is like ordinary bike riding in every respect except one and we will not bother to describe the action column by column. The one way in which speech differs from bike riding is that it is not something we normally think of as being the prerogative of the skillful person. This is in spite of its being one of the most complicated actions we ever perform.

Transference of Sets of Actions

Advice and instructions may aid the mastery of polimorphic actions, but the advice does not comprise a description of what is learned, nor can it replace experience. For a set of instructions covering a polimorphic action to be so complete that it could not be misunderstood by an unsocialized entity, it would need to anticipate all the social circumstances with which the skilled practitioner must cooperate. Neither the advice that can be comprehended by humans, nor the more complex "advice" that can be utilized by computers, amounts to a decontextualized version of a polimorphic action. Because societies cannot be simulated, all abilities below the heavy horizontal line in figure 5.2 can be transferred *only* through socialization. To learn how to interact with a society, one has to interact with that very society. We might call this the "irreplaceability thesis."

Social capabilities, like oral cultures, survive within the continued social activity of those who practice them. Social capabilities cannot be "dried out," like soup, ready to be reconstituted when immersed in the proper social context; they cannot hibernate; they can only die. That is why skills and languages disappear—barring reinvention (MacKenzie and Spinardi 1995; Pinch, Collins, and Carbone 1996).

The formula for a mimeomorphic action, on the other hand, provided it is not impossibly complex, can be inscribed in temporarily decontextualized form, and is therefore transferable in a more straightforward way. A set of mimeomorphic actions can be transferred between human contexts without being extinguished; they are "decontextualizable." We can find transferable descriptions of mimeomorphic actions in written texts, formulas, graphical plots, computer programs, and electronic or mechanical systems. The difference between polimorphic actions and mimeomorphic actions, however, is not the difference between what is "inside" humans and what is "outside." We can, as we have explained, *internalize* a set of mimeomorphic actions.

Just because the behavior associated with mimeomorphic actions can be described and stored outside of a social context, it does not follow that all mimeomorphic actions can be learned outside of social contexts. It is humans that learn to do actions, and humans have certain abilities and limitations that relate to their cognition and physiology rather than to the nature of the action itself.

There are, *then*, *"simple* mimeomorphic actions" and "complex mimeomorphic actions." Examples of repertoires of simple mimeomorphic actions include such things as making Y-O-U in semaphor or marching across a parade ground. Humans can master and even internalize repertoires of simple mimeomorphic actions away from what one might call "the scene of the action"—that is, such a repertoire of behaviors can be learned by reference to some formulaic representation, away from the location of its applications. For example, the chanting of the multiplication table—something that humans can learn as a drill—can be learned in the classroom and usefully applied outside the classroom (*pace* Lave 1988).

An example of a set of complex mimeomorphic actions is bike balancing. Even if the formula is already known to engineers, our brains are not fast enough to cope with learning to bike balance by applying the formula; normally, therefore, we learn bike balancing on a bike. Nevertheless, in contrast to the problem of simulating societies, we could build a bike balancing simulator—something like an aircraft simulator—and learn to balance a bike without ever having sat on one. It just happens that no one thinks this a worthwhile thing to do.

Simulators

The trouble with simulators is that they have to reproduce a repertoire of complex mimeomorphic actions that is the complement of what the learner has to master, and so a considerable effort of formulation is required to build them. For example, building an aircraft simulator is, in principle, something like building an autopilot. This is thought to be worthwhile only when there is a lot at stake. Given that one might drown in a canoe, one day it might just be thought worthwhile to try to build a canoeing-down-rapids simulator.

It is possible to build simulators without being able to express in a symbolic form what one is trying to simulate. Just as with mechanization, clever engineering might be an easier route. Thus to build a canoeing-down-rapids simulator, it might be easier to put a fixed canoe in a fast-flowing variable stream of water rather than computerize the whole thing as in an aircraft simulator. One can also be lucky enough to find simulators already in existence: For some aspects of surgery, animals are naturally occurring simulators for human beings.

Where simulation is not available, the only way for humans to learn sets of complex mimeomorphic actions is, as we have said, through apprenticeship in the context of use. It is the fact that repertoires of mimeomorphic actions are often learned in the same way as polimorphic actions that makes it so easy to confuse the two; the crucial point is, however, that polimorphic actions cannot be learned except through socialization or apprenticeship—mimeomorphic actions can be learned in other ways.

Conclusion

We have shown that there are three basic ways of learning to carry out an action competently. Polimorphic actions are learned through embedding within society. Simple mimeomorphic actions *can* be mastered by learning a set of body movements that can be rehearsed away from the scene of the action itself; what one might call a *drill*. More complicated disjunctive mimeomorphic actions cannot be mastered this way because they are too complex for humans to cope with; our memories are too small, our processing speed is too slow, our calculating abilities are too

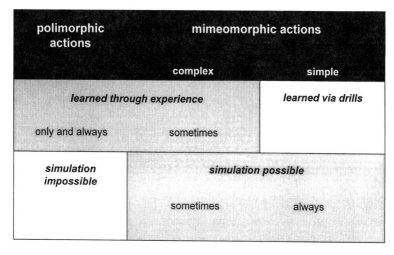

Figure 5.3
Complex and simple mimeomorphic actions

limited. *Repertoires of complex mimeomorphic actions* are usually mastered in the same way as are polimorphic actions—through practice and apprenticeship within society. Under some circumstances, however, they can be mastered through the use of simulators. The relationships are set out in figure 5.3.

Previous analyses have often worked well when the object has been to understand humans. In that case, it is sensible to lump sets of complex mimeomorphic actions along with polimorphic actions because in both cases human mastery rests upon tacit knowledge.[8] Where, however, the question is about the potential replacement without loss of humans by

8. Steven Turner's (1994) analysis of the notion of tacit knowledge suggests that it is a catchall for that which we do not yet understand. Turner may be right, regarding some uses of the term. He is, however, wrong to suggest that the idea of tacit knowledge is vacuous *because* it cannot be reduced to simple components. Turner has turned the problem on its head. Case studies have shown that knowledge maintenance and transfer cannot be reduced to matters of information (or habit) and have thus revealed that some notion like tacit knowledge—which works at the level of the collectivity—is needed if we are to understand the world. Turner's approach would dispose equally of the whole project of sociology, which rests upon the notion of culture or forms of life as the basis of the differences we see between one society and another; analyses of the consequences of these differences does not have to be held in abeyance until some reductionist program

machines, the partition needs to be put in a different place. The crucial partition is not to be located by dividing up what humans can actually do, but by considering what they might be able to do by calculation if only they were as good at processing as are computers or potential computers. If this question is asked, we find that all mimeomorphic actions, complicated or simple, lie on the opposite side of the partition from all polimorphic actions. However powerful a processor is employed, a polimorphic action cannot be mimicked by an unsocialized entity without loss. Confusion is caused, as we have pointed out, by the fact the method by which sets of complex mimeomorphic actions are mastered is often the same as that by which polimorphic actions are mastered; sets of complex mimeomorphic actions *feel like* social capabilities.

---

has been fulfilled. If natural science operated in this way, it would never have started. In this chapter we decompose tacit knowledge into some of its components, without losing sight of the nonreduced aspects of that component associated with polimorphic actions.

6

Writing

Writing a Love Letter

The use of new concepts and terms, like any other skill, needs practice. In analyzing types of writing we clarify some concepts, reveal some applications, and, using our new theory, discover some less than obvious relationships.

In certain societies, a "romantic relationship" sometimes involves the writing of letters from one party to another, in which love and affection is expressed. This is especially likely to happen at the beginning of a relationship, when the bond is being formed, or during a period of enforced absence from the loved one. Somehow, sometime, we learn that there is an action associated with romantic love that is called "writing love letters." We become familiar with love letters in works of fiction or autobiography or, perhaps, in the company of school friends. We are talking of societies such as those of modern Europe, and of the sort of love letters that are written by the literate middle classes. We are talking of the sort of love letters of which several are written in sequence—a sequence that might be bound with a ribbon and stored in an attic, to be rediscovered years later. This kind of literary cliché is part of what gives us our idea of what, in this society, love letters should be like. Writing love letters may be an open action, but it is still an action that is heavily bound up in the constraints of convention—it is polimorphic.

In our society it is hard even to imagine writing love letters in any way except as a polimorphic action. Suppose one could purchase standardized love letters from a "love letter shop." If it were discovered that one's apparently personal letters were, in reality, mass produced, then the beloved would feel cheated. Indeed, it is hard to imagine the existence of institutions such as love letter shops because they would not fit with the institution of love letters as we understand it. (As always, there are exceptions to such a characterization: for example, when one sends a Shakespearean sonnet to one's beloved, one is availing oneself of a mass-produced item, though one could say that the individuality was expressed in the choice of sonnet and in the commitment to the sentiment. Our strategy is not to allow exceptions to divert us from the task of characterizing types of actions in general.)

In the same way, one would not really have written love letters if each letter in a series contained the same words; this would be more likely to be a joke, or a cruel trick, rather than an act of love letter writing. It is, then, almost true to say that creative, context-sensitive variation is intrinsic to the action of love letter writing.[1]

What counts for most of us as "writing a love letter" is not necessarily the same as writing a letter that will have the effect of strengthening the love of another for oneself. Between 1930 and 1937, Gottfried Benn, the German poet, sent identical "love letters" simultaneously to both Elinor Buller and Tilly Wedekind, leading actresses in Berlin and Hanover respectively. Benn wrote to a friend about his love life, saying, "good organization is better than fidelity!" Buller died in 1944, unaware of the trick, but Wedekind discovered the deceit in 1966, ten years after Benn's death, with the publication of his correspondence. Wedekind wrote in her memoirs that when the news broke and a newspaper published a photograph of Buller, she remarked: "I am always happy when my rivals are so beautiful. It would be an affront to my dignity if they were not." It is likely that Wedekind was making the best of a bad situation—it cannot be nice to discover that a personal message is not so personal after all.

"Love," as we understand it within our conventions, is *not* the same as good organization, though perhaps the point could be argued. But

---

1. Here is the exception to this characterization: If either author of this book had a lover who was interested enough to read it, they might receive from the lover a series of identical letters cleverly expressing not only love, but, inter alia, a deep interest in the book—especially now that this note has been written. (Alas, it is unlikely to come about!)

whatever conclusion is reached, none of these concerns mean that there is no such thing as the type of formative action called "love letter writing"; indeed it is the recognizability of the existence of this type of formative action (or institution) that provides the background without which there could be no argument in the first place.

Cyrano, Christian, and Roxane

We can continue to practice our new theory with another well-known example drawn from fiction. In the story of Cyrano de Bergerac by Edmond Rostand, Cyrano writes love letters on behalf of another.[2] Cyrano is in love with Roxane, the target of the letters, but fears that he is too ugly to have his love reciprocated. He agrees to be Christian's agent, in the matter of love letter writing, which suits the inarticulate but handsome Christian well. At the same time, Cyrano uses Christian as his agent in the matter of lovemaking—a far less satisfactory arrangement. Who was engaged in authentic love letter writing, Cyrano, Christian, or neither?

In the story, Cyrano is in love with Roxane and his letters express that love; he writes them as though he is writing on his own behalf. That he conspires to make them appear to have originated elsewhere does not seem to affect the nature of his action. We can say that Cyrano was writing love letters.

But what if Cyrano had not been in love with Roxane? Let us assume that he would have been capable of writing the same prose without having the same feelings for Roxane. First, let us suppose he was in love with someone else and imagined he was writing to her even though the letter was addressed to Roxane.[3] Again, it would seem he was writing love letters. But now suppose Cyrano had never known love but,

2. (Rostand 1942). The story of Cyrano has been modernized as "Roxanne," a film starring Steve Martin. A similar theme is to be found in the short story "Letters of Betrayed Love," by Isabel Allende (1991, pp. 191–200) and in Gabriel Garcia Marquez's *Love in the Time of Cholera* (1988, pp. 171–172). We are grateful to Judith Turbyne for bringing these references to our attention, and to a number of graduate students in the Bath Science Studies Centre for helpful discussion of the points.

3. This is the case with Florentino Ariza, the hero of Garcia Marquez's story.

notwithstanding, had the skill to write the prose? We may imagine he had read the relevant literature and poetry and had frequented the society of those who did know love.[4] In other words, Cyrano would have understood the institution of love and love letters even though he had never felt the individual emotion himself. In this case it is difficult to identify the action *token* correctly even though there is still no doubt at all about the action *type*.

It is still less clear whether Christian was writing love letters. Christian engaged an agent, Cyrano, to write letters on his behalf. Cyrano could express the emotions that Christian knew ought to be expressed. Christian knew what a love letter was—he understood the form of life quite enough to recognize that his own efforts were failures. He could sit down with the intention of writing a love letter, but his results were not likely to be successful; to know all this, Christian had, once more, to understand the action type. We have to say then, that Christian could write a love letter, in the sense that one who knows the rules can play chess, but that he could not write a love letter in the sense that a beginner "can't play chess to save his life." We are not now analyzing Christian's failed attempts, however, but his successes achieved through Cyrano's agency. Are these properly described as "Christian writing love letters"?

In chapter 4 we introduced the notion of an "action cascade." An action cascade looks like an action tree, but some of the elements are carried out by agents of the actor who initiates the cascade. There are many cases of action in which we cause an action to be completed by others, and yet we still speak naturally of the action being carried out by the initiator. To take an example from within the form of life of romantic love, we might send flowers to our beloved via Interflora. In this case we do nothing except make the phone call, yet we would refer to it as sending flowers. To move closer to the case at hand, we might decide that we were so poor at expressing ourselves that instead of composing our own prose we would send a letter, as in our earlier example, consisting largely

---

4. Many mistakes are made through failing to distinguish between individual competence and embedding within a society. For example, those who are unable to use their bodies may still come to understand concepts that are related to the style of embodiment of the majority of the members of the embedding society (Collins 1996).

of an undisguised Shakespeare sonnet. Here we would, as it were, be using William Shakespeare as our agent, but we would still be writing a love letter. Our choice of sonnet and our commitment to the sentiments together express the feelings just as surely as our choice of words in the case of the composition of individual sentences; it is just that the chunks of English language we choose are larger. We would be engaged, in this case, in an *occasioned polimorphic action*, where the choice of behaviors was constrained, but still socially situated. (In our earlier example the parliamentary voter could press only one of three buttons to express a choice; here we can choose from a larger but still limited set of existing pieces of prose).

Following this line of inquiry further, we come to the sending of a preprinted Valentine card. This, it seems, is no longer sending a love letter, for the standardized greeting in such a card is not intended to express deep and individual feelings. Sending a Valentine card is an action type best described as sending a "love token" because the words are not important—the token with its stylized phrases might easily be replaced by a card without any words at all, or by the flowers sent via Interflora. (Token here is being used in a different sense to the way we use it in the phrase "action token.") Sending a love token, then, is not sending a love letter even though it is an expression of affection.

Writing a love letter involves a choice of words designed to express individual emotions in a specific context. But even if we agree that love letters were being sent to Roxane, it is still not clear whether we should assign the responsibility to Christian. It depends, perhaps, upon the extent to which he edited the chunks of words expressed by Cyrano. If he gave Cyrano the mission, "Say things to Roxane that will get her into my bed," then we might say he was not sending love letters but delegating Cyrano to act as his pimp. If, however, he said to Cyrano, "These are the feelings I have for Roxane, express them for me" or even, "Let me see what you have written and we will send if it says what I feel," then we might say he was writing authentic love letters using Cyrano as his agent. The condition is that Cyrano expresses feelings that Christian might recognize within himself. Here the case is different to that of Cyrano, for Christian *might* know only that to get a woman belonging to this society into one's bed it is necessary to send her certain written signs; he might simply engage an agent to send the signs. So, in spite of our best analysis, it seems that to know whether Christian was sending love letters we have to know what he felt for Roxane, and that to know whether Cyrano was sending love letters we have to know whether he felt love for anyone at all.

Because we are not concerned with assigning responsibility to individuals, or answering questions about true love or the authenticity of individual actors, we can leave many questions unanswered while still making satisfactory progress. To make progress we do not have to find out the true facts about either Christian's or Cyrano's internal states— all we have to know is that there is a form of life within which love letters can be written and within which Christian and Cyrano either might or might not be ascribed with responsibility. The very ability to have this discussion, even though we cannot bring it to a conclusion, is an affirmation of the existence of that action type called writing love letters.[5]

That Roxane falls out of love with Christian as soon as she finds out about the subterfuge also does not affect the analysis. What Roxane has discovered is that Christian is a liar and, furthermore, that he does not have the literary abilities she believed him to possess. She has discovered that "Christian could not write a love letter to save his life." It is this ability that Roxane prizes above all others. (Apparently it is the only thing she requires from a lover!)[6] That Roxane prizes this ability shows us that she understands the conventions of love letter writing. Roxane's reactions become one more piece of evidence for the existence of the formative action of love letter writing in our society.

5. Collins (1983) has argued that lies are just as meaningful in terms of indicating the nature of a society as truths. To be able to tell a successful lie rests upon understanding what counts as a truth. To be able to recognize the class lies-truths, and distinguish it from the class of absurdities, jokes, mistakes, and so forth is to understand the society and its corresponding action types.

6. Georgina Rooke has pointed out that this is a rather uncharitable gloss. Roxane engages in an exchange of letters with Cyrano, and therefore may be said to have got to know him quite well through a social interaction, albeit one mediated by the written word. This is not the case, however, for the lovers described by Garcia Marquez (1988), who each employ the same scribe to compose and write their letters for them.

What we have done so far is to illustrate the way the notion of formative actions rescues us from some typical problems associated with action and to indicate how we might refer to the institutions and conventions associated with an action in order to classify it. (In this case we have shown why we think love letter writing is a polimorphic action.) We have distinguished the problem of individual authenticity from the existence of a formative action type and we have distinguished different types of competence. On the one hand there is the ability to perform an action token (or to pretend to perform such a token while acting inauthentically); on the other hand there is the ability to understand and recognize what constitutes the successful performance of an instance of an action type. Being able to appreciate an action is not the same as being able to carry it out, though both are skills in their own way.

The Love Letter Action Tree

Now let us look at the lower branches of the love letter-writing tree. One lower level action is writing itself; getting the words onto the page seems to belong low in the action tree. As we have said, action trees are always polimorphic at the higher levels and (nearly) always mimeomorphic at the lower levels. Is there a "transition point" between polimorphic actions and mimeomorphic actions in the love letter action tree?

Unfortunately, transition points between action morphicities are hard to find. It would be easier if writing worked in a straightforward way: if it were the case that one first "decided" on the words and then wrote them down in the one way possible—an image carried over, perhaps, from the days of scribes—there could be context-sensitive actions all the way down the action tree to the point at which inscription begins, then mimeomorphic actions to the point where action ends. It turns out, however, that writing is a more complex business than that.

First, writing a love letter is different from other types of writing, in that one can be more creative than the language would normally allow. Should one be involved in a certain type of relationship, one might write words such as "snuggledumpling," "lambypiekins," and "coochy-squeezems," which do not have standard spellings. It might be argued that these words are assembled from standard parts, but it is possible to be still more inventive in love letter writing. One might, for example, go in for a bit of "phonetic spelling" (Ah reely reely lurve yoo), or some readily understood nonsense with a touch of studied ambiguity (needle, nidle, nooky noo, how I want to comfort you). Here the choice and arrangement of symbols in the invented words is to some extent open (mee weely weely luv yu; niddle, noddle, nooky, nee, I hope you want to comfort me).[7]

Setting the special features of love letters aside, a more careful examination of the process of writing in general shows that it is a mistake to attribute a morphicity too hastily. We now look more closely at some types of writing, starting with handwriting and moving on to typing.

Hands, Fonts, and Actions

Learning How to Write

Learning to write involves, at the very least, mastering the mimeomorphic actions required to reproduce the equivalent of the 100 or so symbols found on the typewriter keyboard. Preferred teaching styles, as represented in teaching manuals, have changed over the years. Early manuals sought to fix many action parameters.[8] Alfred Fairbank's (1961) *A Handwriting Manual,* first published in 1931, goes to some length to prescribe "pen-direction," position of the body, and "pen-hold." Setting aside the subject matter, we might almost be reading a coaching manual aimed at the golf swing; control of nearly every muscle in the body is demanded.

Pen-direction must be adjusted correctly to the appropriate pen . . . held so that the pen-shaft is pointed away from the right shoulder in the direction of the right forearm (but ascending), whilst the elbow is held lightly and naturally away from the side of the body. A more precise demonstration of the pen-direction is to hold the pen . . . with its edge at about 45° to the writing line of the paper. . . . The paper should be squarely placed before the demonstrator but slightly to the right of the center of the body, and the writing lines should be parallel with the edge of the desk. . . . If a child, seated at his desk but without a pen in hand, placed the fingers of the right hand naturally and easily upon the fingers of the left hand, the left hand being upon the desk and the palms prone, the right forearm would probably be found to be in the direction to give the pen-angle. . . . Every attention

7. Cyrano was better at it.
8. Cf. Foucault 1977, p. 152.

should be given to posture so that it is natural, healthy, confident, comely, and comfortable. The child should sit erect, with level shoulders parallel to the desk. His feet should be placed firmly in front of him on the floor or foot-rest. Both forearms should rest lightly on the desk to within a short distance of the elbows, one forearm being balanced by the other. The chest should not press against the desk. The body should not be curved or turned, nor the head bent over sideways, nor inclined unduly forward. . . . a child's eyes should be from 12 to 14 inches from the writing. . . . The left hand of the child should hold the sheet or exercise book in position and raise the paper when each line is completed. If, where lines are long, the paper is moved to the left at least once after each line is begun, the poise of the head will be less disturbed. . . . As the writing proceeds, the right forearm, which is oblique in relation to the body and to the edge of the desk, should travel a parallel course: that is, it should maintain continuously the same angle to body and desk. The right hand should not swing round, with the elbow as pivot: rather the shoulder should be the pivot and the whole forearm move outwards. . . . The modern orthodox pen-hold is to have the pen between the thumb and first finger, and to hold it in place by the tip of the thumb at the side of the pen, the tip of the first finger above, and the top of the second finger bent at an angle to the pen-shaft and supporting the pen by its side. The third finger is against the second, and the fourth (little finger) against the third. (pp. 28–31)

In Fairbank's account, then, the formation of a letter or word is most definitely a *special singular mimeomorphic action,* whereas inscribing English is going to be a *special disjunctive mimeomorphic action* with a separate but fully prescribed set of behaviors for each sign.

David Wray, writing half a century later in 1987, wants to teach the children more than just how to move their hands and arms for producing the letters.[9] He is also eager to make the children appreciate the role of written texts in our culture. He concentrates less on the fixing of every parameter, believing that the position of the hand, knowledge of the writing instrument, knowledge of the letter shapes, and so forth can be learned within other activities such as drawing.

Wray distinguishes a number of stages. From the age of four, children pick up writing-related skills through drawing. These include how to hold a pen or pencil. Through scribbling, children learn that writing goes in lines across the page and that it uses letters and words that may be familiar from other places. They also begin to learn that writing is about passing on messages. Subsequently, children can trace over the teacher's writing with a pencil. Later the child should copy rather than trace. A

9. We picked this writing primer arbitrarily.

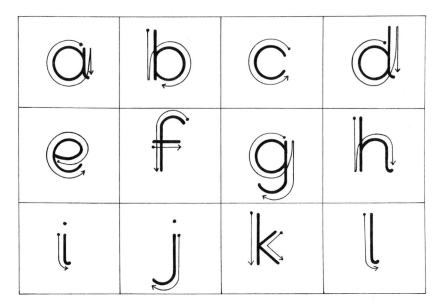

Figure 6.1
Lettering movements. From David Wray, *Writing* (Leamington Spa, U.K.: Scholastic Publications, Ltd., 1987).

beginning may be made if the teacher writes dotted letters asking the children to join up the dots. The teacher can also guide the children's hands in the shapes of letters, perhaps using a sand tray, and can allow the children to get to know the shapes of letters by tracing their fingers over wooden or other models. They should learn to start tracing in the right place and continue in the correct direction. Wray also suggests the use of sheets of handwriting exercises, as well as of computer programs that draw selected letters slowly on the screen.

In spite of Wray's more relaxed approach, there can be no doubt that he, like Fairbank, wants the children's actions of forming the letters to be mimeomorphic. The child is expected to learn specific movements for each type of letter (see figure 6.1), and to make a specific type of movement when asked to produce a specific letter. At this stage of learning, the teacher would be delighted if the pupil could produce identical hand movements corresponding to each letter each time, though the movements of fewer muscles are now specified, and the area of indifference to the direction of the pen and so forth has widened. We see, then, *special*

Figure 6.2
Children's copying of letters and numbers.

mimeomorphic action becoming *casual mimeomorphic action*. We do not claim that we can always say whether every action is on this or that side of this borderline, only that some actions are clearly of one type and some are clearly of another. The standard modern golf swing and Fairbank's version of writing are clear examples of special mimeomorphic actions; Wray's version of writing is nearer to a casual mimeomorphic action. (See figure 6.2 for some examples of five-year-old children copying numbers and letters.)

The child who learns how to write under these two regimes learns, then, a set of mimeomorphic actions. The same seems to hold for adults who learn a new "hand" (style of lettering). They too will try hard to repeat a set of specific movements in order to form the letters of the hand in question. Manuals on calligraphy, like elementary school primers, concern themselves with tracing and copying model letters (figure 6.3). Calligraphy manuals are also concerned with position and angle of the writing hand. For instance, *The Little Manual of Calligraphy*, by Charles Pearce (1981 p. 10), advises the novice as follows:

Sit comfortably at a table in a room where there are likely to be few disturbances. Hold the drawing board at an angle, either resting in the lap against the table, or else, propped up on the table at a suitable angle. If the eyes are kept vertically

Figure 6.3
Copying model letters. From Charles Pearce, *The Little Manual of Calligraphy* (New York: Taplinger, 1981).

above the hand during writing, it will be easier to judge the quality of the letters and the rhythm being achieved. . . . Different styles of writing will demand different pen angles, but whatever the individual style, the angle will remain constant within it.

There are differences between the child learning how to write and the adult learning a new hand. The very young child will not necessarily understand the relation of the drilled bodily movement to the formative action of "writing the alphabet in a recognizable and standardized way"; such a child is learning a repertoire of bodily movements, perhaps with no intention deeper than pleasing the teacher. The full cultural meaning of language is not understood prior to the action's being mastered (though Wray, as opposed to Fairbank, obviously wants to teach some of this). When learning a new hand, however, it is certain that the adult understands the meaning of writing and knows what it is to master a script before being able to control bodily movements to the standards of the manual. Thus the relationship between the intention and the drill is likely to be different in the two cases.

Writing as Marching and Writing as Dancing

Tracing and copying letters is only one type of writing. We can distinguish at least six forms of writing by hand: the child's script, the adult's script(s), the signature, the calligrapher-copyist's script, the calligrapher-designer's script, and the calligrapher-illuminator's script. These scripts differ in their combinations of morphicities.

The Child's Script   We have already shown that learning how to write the letters and numbers is in the first instance learning a set of mimeomorphic actions. That is to say, it is normal within "Western culture" for children to be expected to carry out specific movements with hands and arms in order to produce, as far as possible, exact replicas of model letters and words.[10] The child's script is, then, a *special mimeomorphic action.*

The Adult's Script(s)   Even though Western children are initially required to follow specific models and standards of how to write, at a later stage they are usually expected to develop a personal style of handwriting. Fairbank (1961, p. 15) remarks that "a model [of writing] is but a guide to the beginning of an unknown personal journey, the directions one takes later being a matter of private inclination."

The development of a personal hand can involve complicated negotiations, as there can be a conflict between personal idiosyncrasy and the

---

10. Note that this way of writing is not a "fact of nature," but one of culture and society. Consider the parallel case of grammar. It has been reported that in most Pacific languages it is impossible to be ungrammatical, and there is no language community in which "certain persons are understood to speak with due regard for syntax and certain others betray their lack of education by speaking incorrectly" (Harris 1987, p. 108). We can imagine that some language communities would place equally little emphasis on the precision with which letters have to be traced. (Perhaps, for the child in our culture, the norms and rules governing writing have something of an exemplary role when it comes to accepting that there is a "correct" grammar.)

Note also that there exist (scientific) controversies over which script and style should be taught first to elementary school children. For instance, Suen (1983) reports on the controversy in the United States over the question of whether children should be taught a manuscript style in which letters are separated, or a cursive style in which letters are joined. As we shall see later, the introduction of "intelligent" script readers can influence such debates.

demand for legibility. The outcome of this negotiation is the *hand* in which the adult writes. The idea of personal handwriting demands that we make yet another distinction in our types of action. Adult handwriting is a mimeomorphic action, as it is expected to be constant once it is formed; someone who was to develop a new hand for him- or herself every day, or every week, would be regarded as odd. Nevertheless, one's handwriting is also expected to be different from that of others. We already know that the notion of doing something in the "same way" each time requires a reference to context and we know that *disjunctive mimeomorphic actions* vary with context. To understand personal handwriting under this scheme requires that we treat the individual as a context; each person's way of writing a word is expected to remain the same with respect to him- or herself (singular) while varying (disjunctive) with respect to individuals. To put this in more commonsensical terms, we have a distinction between *self-copying* and *other-copying* mimeomorphic actions. With self-copying actions the standard is personal, while other-copying mimeomorphic actions follow a public standard.[11]

To sum up, in our society most children learn to write any particular word as a *special* (a bit more casual in Wray's version) *singular* (other-copying) *mimeomorphic action.*[12] Adults write any particular word as a *casual disjunctive,* with respect to individuals (self-copying), *mimeomorphic action.* We have speculated that there is an in-between stage. In this stage the Western child is not expected to control the movements of the pen quite so carefully, and is allowed to produce a more "sloppy" effect so long as it is still legible: This is the *casual mimeomorphic action* out

---

11. Jenkins (1994) shows that this terminology can also be applied to the golf swing. Different golfers and coaches believe in the correctness of swings modeled on those of one or another great player such as Hogan, Nicklaus, or Faldo. Whichever of these models is accepted, the golf swing is thought of as an other-copying action—there is one and one only standard swing. There are, however, schools of opinion that think the swing should not be other-copying but primarily self-copying. Some teachers think that the student should be taught to perfect a swing that fits the pupil's particular physical and mental endowment and that the job of the golf coach is first to discover the best style of swing for the pupil and then "maintain" it—that is, continually correct it as, inevitably, it drifts away from the version tailored to the particular pupil.

12. Remember that *words,* as opposed to any particular word, are written disjunctively.

of which a personal adult hand can develop. This description is, of course, historically and culturally specific. Victorian clerks in Britain, seen as cogs in a bureaucratic machine, were expected to write a uniform "Copperplate"—once more a *special singular* other-copying *mimeomorphic action*—even though they were adults.

Turning back to the typical modern case, adults tend to have more than one hand or style at their disposal. At the very least, we can all write in block letters when the purpose is a note to the milkman or some such. Some of us have a broader repertoire still: for example, one of the authors of this book (Kusch) was taught to write in the now outdated Sütterlin script—used widely in the German-speaking world until the 1950s—and learned Gabelsberger stenography in order to read manuscripts by turn-of-the-century German philosophers; the other author (Collins) was taught a calligraphic hand during art lessons at school. Thus there are two levels at which the mimeomorphic action of writing is disjunctive. Not only is our normal personal hand individually distinctive, but we may choose different hands for different contexts. To give an unfortunate example, the legibility of our handwriting is sometimes related to the relative status of writer and reader; the higher the relative social status of the writer, the fewer concessions he or she has to make to the reader. Medical doctors' relationship with pharmacists is, perhaps, a good example.

Finally, note that there are circumstances when the adult individual is expected *not* to write in his or her own hand: the writer of a Valentine's card is expected to disguise his or her identity by using a different hand but not the public standard: someone who wrote his or her Valentine's cards with a computer or a typewriter (as Kusch did before he came to understand the institution properly) would be regarded as committing a faux pas.

The Signature In some respects, the signature is an ideal type of the adult personal hand. Quintessentially, it does not follow a public standard, but has an individual style. It is more toward the *special* rather than the *casual* end of the spectrum of *mimeomorphic actions* because we try to repeat the same movements of (at least) the hand, wrist, and fingers every time. Making a signature is, then, a *special disjunctive* (self-copying) *mimeomorphic action*.

ARTHUR BAKER
Two calligraphic alphabets
Written with a Coit pen and reduced
Reproduced by courtesy of Dover Publications.

Figure 6.4
Calligraphy.

The Calligrapher-Copyist's Script   Now consider calligraphy alongside "normal" handwriting. Calligraphy is, as Fairbank (1961, p. 13) puts it, "handwriting when considered [as] an art . . . it is a dance of the pen." As with normal handwriting the art of calligraphy has different stages and forms. Calligraphic *copying* can be considered a stage in the acquisition of the complete art of calligraphy. Fairbank calls it "pure calligraphy" since it does not seeks to express the personality of the writer-copyist. This form of calligraphy is *special* other-copying *mimeomorphic action,* and thus structurally similar to the actions that the child is striving for. Figure 6.4 shows examples of calligraphy.

The Calligrapher-Designer's Script   The art of calligraphy also includes the activity of inventing a new script, or modifying and developing an already existing—perhaps "classical"—script. In this case calligraphers are as much designers as copyists: they are designers insofar as they invent/design new scripts and new *types* of letters, but they are copyists when they produce products that use the letter types of the new script

Cambridge St Edinburgh EH1 2ED
tel. 031 228 8882

Figure 6.5
Calligraphy on a restaurant menu.

(figure 6.5). This combination of the polimorphic action of design—an action that requires constant reference to the reception of the design by the social group—and mimeomorphic action is similar to the initial developing and subsequent stabilization of an adult hand.[13]

The Calligrapher-Illuminator's Script   The calligrapher illuminator tries *not to* repeat the same letter twice. Traditionally, the illuminator's task was to paint the initial letter of books, chapters, and pages using a variety of geometrical and decorative shapes, adding scenes, shapes, bodies, and faces (see figure 6.6). The calligrapher who tries to make every single letter token (or several letter tokens) of a given text look different follows the illuminator's lead.[14] In this case, the main feature of the lettering is that it is a polimorphic action—referring to social conventions rather than following a geometrical standard for letter shapes.

The Adventurous Scribe   One last story brings out our major distinction again. Geza Vermes (1994) reports that the "Dead Sea Scrolls"

13. We find a similar relation of a shift from polimorphic to mimeomorphic actions in science and technology (see chapter 8).

14. We cannot demonstrate this convincingly on the basis of a limited corpus of letter-tokens. For a fixed body of examples one can always find a set of rules that includes every instance.

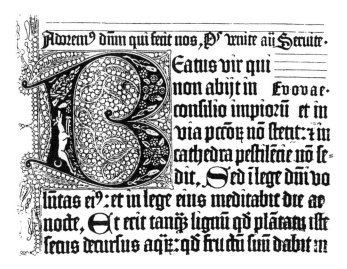

Figure 6.6
The work of the illuminator.

include documents that have been copied from one another by scribes. While medieval Hebrew scriptural manuscripts are "remarkable for their uniformity," divergencies being "scribal errors" or variations in spelling, the scrolls show a great deal of variation. To quote Vermes:

> The startlingly different versions reveal what one scholar has called "insufficiently controlled copying." In my view, the differences may be better explained by attributing a considerable degree of creative freedom to the scribes. Copyists evidently felt free to alter compositions they were reproducing. (p. 12)[15]

15. Vermes says that the scribe of a "Cave 4" Deuteronomy manuscript steered a middle course between the short "Masoretic text" and the long formulation of the Greek "Septuagint," these being works from which a conventional wording might have been adopted. He gives the following example:
Masoretic text: Rejoice o nations with his people. For he shall avenge the blood of his servants and shall take revenge on his enemies.
Greek Septuagint: Rejoice o heavens with him and let all the angels of God worship him. Rejoice o nations with his people and let all the sons of God declare him mighty. For he shall avenge the blood of his sons and shall take revenge and pay justice to his enemies and shall reward them that hate him.
Qumran Cave 4 Fragment: Rejoice o heavens with him and all you "gods" worship him. For he shall avenge the blood of his sons and shall take revenge on his enemies and shall reward them that hate him. (p. 13)

If Vermes is right, what the scribes were doing was certainly polimorphic action. They had in mind the meaning of their words in relation to the social context for which they were writing. Meaningful alterations could not have been effected by those who did not understand the social context. This is quite different from a scribe's freedom to make variations in the shape of letters—*casual mimeomorphic action*. It is also quite different from spelling variations and "scribal errors," which are failures to carry out a *casual mimeomorphic action*. Thus even when the scribe's task is considered, we can see that it can consist of various different types of action. In the medieval tradition, copying Hebrew text would almost certainly be a *special mimeomorphic action;* the exact shape of every letter that the scribe was copying would have significance. In the scrolls of Qumran, we may guess that lettering was not so exact a thing—it was a *casual mimeomorphic action.* And we can now see that even though the idea of scribe initially leads us to think of inscribing words on paper as an essentially mimeomorphic action, there are aspects of scribes' work that have been polimorphic.

The Word Processor
We have treated writing as though the actual words written are chosen independently of the process of writing them down. Sometimes this is not true. It may have been true when the writing surface was such that there was no means of making alterations to an inscription. It may be true now when an author is dictating to another. It may even be true for a small subset of authors who are able to produce well-turned prose at the first attempt, or who do not care whether the prose is well turned or not, but the advent of new writing technologies has allowed more and more alteration of text after the initial inscription. The most recent step is, of course, the word processor. The word processor can make the process of composition integral with the process of inscription, making the transition point on the writing action tree still more elusive.

Writing Summarized
The distinctions made above are summarized in figure 6.7.

In the first part of the chapter we showed how we handle possible confoundings of questions of individual authenticity and questions

	type of mimeomorphic action	type of polimorphic action	type of copying
child	special	-	other-copying
adult	casual	-	self-copying
signature	special	open/playful (in the designing stage	self-copying
calligrapher-copyist	special	-	other-copying
calligrapher-designer	special (as far as tokens are concerned)	open/playful (as far as types are concerned)	self-copying
calligrapher-illuminator	-	open/playful (with respect to every letter-token)	no copying

Figure 6.7
Types of writing.

having to do with formative action types. Our major point is that questions about authenticity make sense only if one initially understands the action types that form the social background. It is not that the difficulty of assigning a motive, or the correct description of an action to an individual, damages the theory; rather that only by accepting the notion of "form of life" and its correlates can questions of proper attribution of intention make sense.

We then moved on to an exploration of the relationship between polimorphicity and mimeomorphicity in the love letter writing action tree, where we discovered that there is no neat transition point between polimorphic and mimeomorphic actions. The way the words of the letter might be put on paper could vary enormously in its morphicity. Many of the types of writing described above might be employed by the love letter writer. Why not use calligraphy? Why not illuminate some letters? The choice of hand is itself part of a polimorphic action, while the employment of the hand itself might or might not have polimorphic aspects. We spent some time practicing the new terminology on varieties of handwriting.

The analysis shows that applying the new theory properly is hard work and that the theory cannot be used carelessly. If one is to understand the nature of action as a precursor to understanding the way different elements of our actions can be replaced by machines, one must look at each action in considerable detail, for actions are not always what they seem to the casual glance. A fitting way of illustrating this is to consider what types of machines might be used to replace or aid writing skills; this is how we start the next chapter.

7

Machine Behavior and Human Action

Speech transcribers, signature-making machines, a machine for writing personalized script, spell checkers, and bibliographic aids—these are the kinds of machines that can help humans write. They are among the behavers that humans use to assist their actions. After examining writing machines, we move on to a typology of machines in general.

Writing Machines

Speech Transcribers
For years we have been promised that the arrival of speech transcribers is imminent. These are machines into which one can speak and have one's spoken words presented in typed form on one's computer screen. For various reasons, the promise has been fulfilled only partially, and the horizon over which we expect to see a fully functional speech transcriber appear recedes as fast as we move toward it.[1] But suppose a fully functioning speech transcriber arrived on the scene tomorrow. How would we use it?

Let us suppose that the transcriber included a grammar checker and a spell checker so that it transformed our messy speech, with all its ahs and uhms, into correctly spelled, grammatically immaculate prose.[2] Let us compare such a speech transcriber with a skilled secretary.

1. For an explanation of this in terms of the nature of the action of speaking see, for example, Collins (1993).
2. We will return to the problems of spell checkers and grammar checkers later in this chapter.

A secretary can understand phrases such as the following: "Go back to that sentence where I mentioned the papers and ask for an additional copy of the one on solar neutrinos." The secretary knows that this is not a piece of speech to be transcribed, but is an instruction for making a transformation of earlier transcribed text. The secretary can find the relevant passage and make the transformation even though the form of transformation is not specified in detail. The secretary will understand the meaning of "additional copy" as "an extra copy" or "a copy of an additional paper," depending on whether the solar neutrino paper has already been mentioned. In short, the secretary is capable of acting with context-sensitive understanding of the text. A speech transcriber will have to do much more than transcribe words in order to be as useful a dictating machine as a secretary.

There are other complexities to the interaction between writing and speech. For at least some writers, the process of writing on a word processor is integral to the process of composition. If the keyboard were to be replaced by speech transcription, the speech transcription tool would, like the human secretary, have to be able to understand when it was meant to transcribe and when it was meant to understand the words as a set of instructions. In addition, it would have to understand and obey a far wider range of instructions than the secretary, and with much greater speed of reaction. The reactions would have to be fast enough to allow several versions of a sentence or paragraph to be tried and rejected at little less than thinking speed.

The speech transcribing tool would, then, have to be able to replace words, replace sections, insert sections, and so forth, by recognizing and following a set of spoken instructions that would have to be no more trouble to utter than is involved in normal backspacing and retyping—and backspacing and retyping is quite easy. It would be nice not to have to sit in one place to do the work, and not to have to maintain one's body and arms stationary in such an awkward, upright position; it would be nice to be able to pace around the room while one's thoughts appeared on the screen, but not at the expense of continually repeating oneself in order to explain exactly how one wanted the last passage reshaped.[3]

---

3. For bad typists, speech transcribers that do a reasonable job and then allow for easy correction of the text at a later stage might still be better than typing from scratch.

Because writing is so complicated, a careful examination of action is necessary if the relationship between humans and machines is to be understood. The polimorphic actions, which cannot be mimicked by machines without alteration of the action, and the mimeomorphic actions, which can, are deeply intermingled in writing. In the case of writing, we tend to think that mimeomorphicity goes higher up the action tree than it does.

Lettering

The ultimate transformation of fully edited words into their form as marks on paper is lower down the action tree. Let us call this "lettering." Even here the actions are sufficiently involved with social institutions to make the substitution of human action with machine behavior much less straightforward than it first seems. Not all lettering consists of mimeomorphic actions—illuminated capitals and illuminated calligraphy rest on polimorphic actions, and we should not expect them to be straightforwardly replaceable by machine behavior.

Even the mimeomorphicity of an action is not a *sufficient* criterion for replacement by machine; it depends upon the social institutions within which the action is embedded. For example, there are sports, such as golf or high-board diving, that depend upon the execution of mimeomorphic actions, and yet replacing the humans by machines in these cases would be to miss the point of the sport. In lettering the same applies: Many cases of the production of mimeomorphic lettering are not candidates for replacement by machine. Calligraphy is sportlike in this respect. Different computer fonts on our computer are in some respects like the different hands or calligraphic scripts that can be mastered by the adult. And yet we do not admire people for their ability to use different fonts, whereas we do applaud or admire the versatile calligrapher. Of course, there is a residue of polimorphic action to be admired in the creative calligrapher, but the point we are making here is that even the mimeomorphic element of calligraphy can be admired when executed by a skillful human. As we explained in the chapter on human competence, there is no straightforward relationship between the value we put on skills and their morphicity.

The importance of the method of production of mimeomorphic script is again clear in those cases where typescript is not an acceptable substitute for handwriting. To send someone a typed love letter would be odd. To send a note of condolence in something other than handwriting would be equally odd. An interesting case encountered by one of the authors concerned a note sent by a university faculty dean informing personnel of the death of a staff member; the note was laser-printed with a font that mimicked human handwriting. One can see what the dean was trying to do, but the fact that the note was not handwritten was taken by many staff to indicate a failure on the part of the dean to understand what we might call "the aesthetics of emotion." Strangely, a handwritten note that had been obviously photocopied would have been more acceptable.

There are opposite cases where writers are expected to avail themselves of machines. Because of its relative illegibility, to distribute a scientific paper to one's peers in handwritten form would nowadays be judged impolite, and to send such a thing to a journal editor would be inappropriate.

The Signature

Another case where machines can replace the pen in only special circumstances is the signature. Making a signature, a quintessentially (self-copying) mimeomorphic act, is a mark of identification; just as bullets show the marks of the gun that fired them, and typewriters have their specific quirks that enable the police to work out which machine was used to type a threatening note, the written signature is, to use the word metaphorically, the "signature" of a particular biological machine—you. Those who forge signatures disguise their biological machinery as that of another. In the normal way, then, it would be inappropriate to use a machine to make your signature, because the test of identity works only if it is the biological you who utters the signature.

One exception to this rule is the signature machines used by banks and other large financial institutions; another is the signature on a banknote; another is the printed facsimiles of signatures to be found on advertising junk mail. In these cases, however, we are not really looking at signatures but at signature tokens (again, "token" is not used here in the sense of "action token"). In the case of the banknote, the exact form of the signature is of no interest to anyone—it must be one of the easiest elements of the banknote to forge. In the case of signature machines, we are substituting the "signature" of a metal mechanism for the signature of the biological machine; it would not matter if the signature produced by the machine exactly matched the signature of the corresponding human, for the signature indicates only that the check was written within the institution that housed the signature machine. The signature machine, then, fulfills the same role as an official seal, rather than that of a human being. In the case of junk mail, it is rather hard to see what the printed signature is for; perhaps some take it as a symbol of personal attention, but surely only the most gullible. In the case of a typed letter, the sender is expected to sign by hand if they mean to show that it has been composed—or at least read—by the sender.

On the other hand, one of the authors once worked in the office of an American senator who owned a different type of signature machine. This was a record-and-playback device into which an ordinary pen could be fixed. If a letter was properly positioned, the metal arm of the device would move the pen in such a way as to reproduce the senator's preprogrammed signature. Here the intention was to deceive the receiver of the letter into thinking that the senator had given more personal attention to the response than was in fact the case. This machine was kept well hidden from visitors to the office, reinforcing the point about the norms associated with signing letters. We see here a machine used to effect a deceit—a case of an inauthentically executed mimeomorphic action. It is interesting that even mimeomorphic actions can be inauthentic. Thus we see that the distinction between authenticity and inauthenticity does not map onto the distinction between polimorphic and mimeomorphic actions.

Is There a Market for a New Kind of Writing Machine?

The senator's signature machine, along with our analysis of lettering, invites the invention of a new kind of word-processor program. Such a machine would learn the character of a writer's hand, through the input of various samples of writing, with the aim of being able to develop a font that reproduces the hand (with various haphazard variations), in response to keyboard input. Allied with a suitable color printer (or even a pen manipulator), this device would produce text that could be hard to distinguish from the handwriting of the typist. A machine such as this would be useful to someone who finds typing much easier than hand-writing, or who finds the keyboard and screen an indispensable element in composition, but who still wants to write personal notes and letters. Admittedly, sending this kind of letter to strangers would involve an element of deceit, while sending it to friends might suggest, like the note sent by the dean, a lack of aesthetic judgment. It is possible, however, that such machines would change the way we think about handwriting. The reception of such a program would make a nice case study in the meaning of "personal" within our society.

Spell Checkers and Bibliography Checkers

We now travel back up the writing tree a little way to discover another feature of the relationship between polimorphicity and mimeomorphicity in the action of writing. Consider spell checkers. Even spelling can be a polimorphic action. Occasionally we want to be adventurous in our spelling, as in our love letter examples or in poetry or some kinds of novel. More problematically, consider that a spell checker will correct the misspelling in antidisestablishmentareanism (a mistake that many humans would miss), and in weerd processor, but not in world processor (which nearly every human would spot). This is because world is cor-rectly spelled though weerd is not. More complicated still, antidisestab-lishmentareanism, weerd processor, and world processor are all spelled just as we want them in this passage of text as it appears in this book, so any corrections the spell checker made would be mistakes. The spell checker would have to understand the whole sense of this passage if it were to spell as well as the typical editor. Thus we value a degree of polimorphicity in our spelling, and because of this it is currently impos-sible to design a spell checker that checks in the same way a human checks.

Compare spelling with entries in the bibliography of an academic book or paper. When it comes to bibliographies, we seem to be interested in standardization and uniformity and not at all concerned with creativity, freedom of expression, or context dependency (except of a very narrow, disjunctive-mimeomorphic sort—i.e., which style for which journal). It would be very unusual for someone to claim that their work is especially valuable because of its sensitive bibliographic response to social circumstance. Thus in the case of bibliographies we do not seem to value polimorphicity at all; it is all mimeomorphicity.

Here is a typical bibliographic warrant offered by a sensitive writer, Steven Shapin (1994, p. xxiii):

> This book uses an economical footnoting and referencing convention identical to that employed by Shapin and Schaffer's *Leviathan and the Air-Pump* and similar to that of Elizabeth Eisenstein's *The Printing Press as an Agent of Change.*

As can be seen, the stress is on convention and similarity to previous usage by self and others, whereas such an author is normally concerned to emphasize creative features of his or her texts. An author who wrote that his or her referencing system was idiosyncratic and should not be adopted by others would not have understood the point of referencing as it is valued in our society. For this reason we would predict that referencing conventions will converge and that eventually referencing that is not aided by machine will become rare. We predict that references will come to be stored in standard databases, that there will be programs that format them for different house styles, that the number of house styles will rapidly diminish, and that all these changes will be welcomed by almost everyone, and will *not* be seen as an example of the growing tyranny of machines, even by "neo-Luddites." This, of course, is not a particularly adventurous prediction since the trend is well under way.

What Machines Can Do

Some of these complexities can be understood within a more general framework. What kinds of machines are there in the world? There are at least two ways of typologizing machines, the first is according to what they do, and the second is according to how they work. We deal first with what machines do.

Machines are of three kinds:

1. *Tools:* Machines can amplify our ability to do what we can already do—let us call such machines "tools." A hammer is a tool; a mechanical digger is a tool; a word processor is a tool; a medical diagnostic help system is a tool.

2. *Proxies:* Machines can replace us by doing what we already do (perhaps better than we can do it)—let us call such machines "proxies."

A rope tied round a bollard to hold a boat still is a proxy; a thermostat is a proxy; the control belonging to a radar-controlled gun is a proxy; a computer program that integrates mathematical functions is a proxy; an expert system for medical diagnosis is a proxy.

3. *Novelties:* Machines can do types of things that we could never do without them—let us call such machines "novelties." A high bridge is a novelty; an explosive device is a novelty; a fridge-freezer is a novelty; a space rocket is a novelty; a laser is a novelty; a virtual-reality headset is a novelty.

The boundaries between the three categories are, as we have come to expect of these things, less than watertight. The differences are partly a matter of the level of analysis. Consider first the difference between tools and proxies. Between the moment that one presses forward the little lever on a tool such as a mechanical digger, to instruct it to drag the bucket, teeth first, through the earth toward you, and the moment the bucket comes to the end of its travel, the device is acting not as a tool but as a proxy—it is scooping up earth "by itself." When action is broken down into small enough elements, tools become proxies. To take an example from our analysis of writing machines, if one is word processing a document that one intends to present as typescript, from the moment one completes the "print" instruction to the moment the document emerges in the paper tray, the word processor/printer is a proxy; it is typing for one.

On the other hand, we can always turn a proxy into a tool by considering what it does from a vantage point higher up in the action tree—thus, a rope is a tool for our ship-controlling actions, a radar-controlled gun is a tool we use in our war-waging actions, and a word processor is a tool we use in our writing actions.

The general rule is that we can always turn a tool into a proxy by taking a lower vantage point, and we can always turn a proxy into a tool by taking a higher vantage point.

Novelties are only a little more robust. A space rocket can be seen as a tool by standing at a very high level of the tree (it amplifies our ability to travel), and even into a proxy with sufficient determination (it travels for us?). A fridge-freezer, which seems at first sight to be able to do something that no human can do (freeze water), can be said to amplify our ability to preserve food or even, attributing agency, to preserve food for us. Likewise, tools can be seen as novelties (the digger bucket lifts a ton at a time), and so can proxies (a rope can hold a huge ship for ages and ages). Our word processors are innovators, to the extent that they enable us to integrate creative composition and the production of script to an unprecedented extent.

What we count as a tool, a proxy, or a novelty depends then upon our standpoint in the action tree. But this "relativity" rests on something that is not so relative: if correct description of a machine depends on standpoint, there are also incorrect descriptions of machines where the relationship between standpoint and attribution of degree of independence is incorrect. The burden of much of the argument of this book and of previous works is that what have been taken to be proxies should really be thought of as tools. It is easy to mistake tools for proxies because of the ease with which we "repair" the deficiencies of machines and then "attribute" agency to them.[4] This is what we will call "Repair, Attribution, and all That" or "RAT."[5]

RAT: Hiding It, Balancing It, Killing It

Pocket calculators do not "do arithmetic"; they do only a tiny part of arithmetic. We think a pocket calculator does arithmetic after the fashion of a proxy, or even an agent, because we continually repair its errors and attribute high-level arithmetical agency to it. If you pick up a cheap pocket calculator and do the sum "7/11 × 11" you get the answer 6.9999996, but you do not immediately write a letter to the manufacturers telling them that they have sold you a dud calculator. You look at the result and you "see" 7. Seeing 7 where there is only 6.9999996 is part of the work you do in making the interaction between you and the

4. We say nothing here of the morality of the attribution of these terms to machines. Ask the question of the senator's signature machine. Was it a proxy for the senator? One might say "yes" in that it reproduced the senator's signature for him, or one might say "no" because a machine cannot replace a senator in his role as one who distributes his limited personal attention according to the deserts of the cause. The signature machine appears to increase the total of the senator's personal attention; on the other hand, the value of personal attention would seem to be commensurate with its scarcity.

5. See Collins (1996).

calculator look like ordinary arithmetic. If one analyses the process more carefully, one finds that a lot of work is done by the user, both at the input stage and at the output stage.[6]

This work is of the same sort as is needed when one hears the strange accents and intonations of a voice-generating chip uttering a telephone number, or insisting that "a door is a jar" (a phrase frequently evinced by some cars built in the 1980s).[7] Users can turn mangled vocalizations into English words because they can provide enough context to make sense of what such a device is "trying to say." On the input side, voice-operated computers require users to speak in a strange stilted way if they are to work. This is because they *cannot* do the same sort of interpretative, contextualizing work on humans' varying vocalizations that we can do on theirs. The special way of speaking that users have to adopt is equivalent to their being ready to insert an arithmetical sum into the calculator through a keyboard that offers a limited choice of options in the way the sum is expressed.

What one is doing when one sees 6.9999996 as 7 and hears the voice chip as saying ordinary words is known as "repair." The user is repairing the deficiencies of the computer. Insofar as we do such repair work without noticing it, we can easily think of the calculator (voice chip) as doing arithmetic (speaking). It is rather like the process of anthropomorphization. People might attribute human characteristics to their dog, to their car, and to their calculator. This is what we are doing when we say that our calculator is "better at arithmetic than we are." We are doing repair and attribution and all that.[8]

"Hiding the RAT" is the most general principle of computer interface design. The interface is designed so that the user is unaware of how much RAT he or she is putting into the interaction. The way to do this is to have the computer need only the kind of RAT that we are accustomed to using in our everyday lives. In other words, make the interface require

6. See Collins (1990), chap. 5; and Collins (1997).

7. A very well known English riddle goes "When is a door not a door?—When it's ajar" [a jar].

8. The source of the idea of "repair" is the ethnomethodological literature. See, for example, Garfinkel (1967).

only ubiquitous skills. This is called making interfaces "user friendly." It is less a matter of making the interface do skillful things and more a matter of encouraging users to take advantage of the skills they already have.

The examples given in the previous section are like this. Every pre-calculator era arithmetician was already accustomed to approximating, because the logarithm tables and slide rules that they used required even more approximating skills than do calculators. That is why the calculator's mistakes are so easy to repair, and why it is so easy to attribute arithmetician's skills to them. Ubiquitous skills are transparent; one does not notice that one has them. The repair of broken speech patterns is another ubiquitous skill. One of the things that designers are doing, as programs become more user friendly, is to make their programs touch our culture in places where the skills of repair are already in place (Collins 1990, chap. 7).

One design mistake is to think that a computer that thoroughly hides the RAT does not need RAT at all. This kind of mistake led, for example, to the overblown claims for the power of expert systems such as auto-mated medical diagnosticians—for example, MYCIN. Such mistakes happen when computer enthusiasts fail to understand how much work and skill humans put into their day-to-day interactions and into their interactions with machines. If one does not notice how skill-laden is ordinary social life, one may think that a system with which people can interact easily is a social creature. But it is not a social creature unless the pattern of skill use is roughly symmetrical between all parties. Once again, the asymmetry is easily seen in systems that involve speech, but careful analysis will show its presence in nearly all computer-human interactions.[9] Only in special cases is symmetry achievable with current or immediately foreseeable machines.

To move the correct attribution of agency up the tree, the RAT has to be "balanced." At the top of the tree, human interaction, and human-machine interaction, involve a lot of interpretation and repair. "Balancing the RAT" means building devices that are as good at RAT as are humans,

9. For a hilarious account of "unbalanced RAT" (our term) in automated photo-copiers, see Suchman (1987).

so that the burden of repair is distributed evenly between both parties in an interaction, even when one is a machine. In current computer-human interactions nearly all the RAT is done by the humans.[10] Only if the RAT is balanced could the machine be said to be taking the place of a socialized human being working at the top end of the action tree. Only a conversationalist that could balance the RAT could pass a Turing test in which the interrogator asked questions (in misspelled English full of puns and so forth) that required for their rectification the sort of understanding gained through socialization. No ordinary balanced-RAT interchange can be managed unless, one way or another, we put social knowledge into computers.

There is another way of balancing the RAT; this is to eliminate the need for it—what one might call "killing the RAT." Machines can take the role of ordinary, socialized, human beings without being members of society under some circumstances. The circumstances are that ordinary humans beings want to do things that could be done without the skills, ways of conceptualizing the world, and ways of acting and speaking that are normally mastered with socialization. This way of doing things is, of course, mimeomorphic action.

The Proper Attribution of Agency

To paraphrase the earlier argument about calculators in terms of the ideas set out above, we can say that agency is correctly attributed to calculators only when the vantage point is low in the action tree. Careless optimists, however, continue to talk and think of calculators as proxies, or even agents, even when they are seeing them from much higher in the tree—the attribution of agency "slips up the tree" as it were.[11] Careless optimists think they are seeing high-level agents when they are seeing only low-level proxies, and they maintain the illusion by repair and attribution.

10. This is not to say that computers and other machines cannot do various bits of repair such as elementary spell checking, but as we have explained above, they fall well short of human competence because of the polimorphic element of spelling.

11. It could be said that this is what Drew McDermott (1981) was getting at in his article, "Artificial Intelligence and Natural Stupidity."

Other supposed proxies simply do not work because their users are unable to supply the necessary amount of RAT. Thus there simply are no satisfactory medical diagnostic expert systems, only diagnostic help systems.[12] Help systems are meant to aid skilled users, whereas expert systems are meant to replace expert users. Installing an expert system within a culture that repairs its errors defeats the object—it becomes a help system and is better designed with that goal in mind. Furthermore, in the circumstances of most hospitals, the mistakes of diagnostic expert systems are readily detected precisely because the systems are monitored by skillful doctors. To find circumstances in which a diagnostic system will work as intended, on must find a location where it is the only resource. Hartland (1993) found that a heart-disease system was never used in city hospitals but was used in a remote rural hospital to refer patients to specialists, because at the rural hospital a high level of "false positives" (with the associated worry and waste of resources) was more acceptable than a small number of false negatives (with fatal consequences), and there was no skilled doctor on hand able to do better.

Machines as Proxies

In this book we are interested in machines as proxies. We have almost nothing to say about novelties, and little to say about tools except that they are often mistaken for proxies. We are interested, in short, in where current and foreseeable machines can replace us—where they can do what we are already doing. And our argument is that machines can only be proxies where whatever we want to bring about can be brought about through mimeomorphic actions.

We can now see one way in which this makes sense. Machines are turned from tools to proxies by going down the tree; but, of course, as we go down the tree we specify actions ever more narrowly, such that they tend toward mimeomorphicity. There is less "relativity" than we first thought! More narrowly specified elements of the tree tend to be mimeomorphic and therefore tend to be more available to replacement by mechanical proxies.

12. See Lipscombe (1989). Or systems that work because the organizations adjust to them in various ways (Berg 1997).

The section on writing machines shows that even this relationship is not straightforward. We discovered that speech transcription, as carried out by a human secretary, contained polimorphic actions. We found that typing, when it was an element within creative composition, was intimately tied up with polimorphic activities. We found that spelling could contain a polimorphic element. We found that a person's signature, quintessentially mimeomorphic though it is, could not be reproduced by a machine without turning into something like a "seal of office," or becoming a kind of forgery (as where the senator used his signing machine to give the impression that his own biological mechanism had produced the mark). These, however, are caveats and qualifications rather than councils of despair. A speech transcriber could be a reasonable proxy for a copy-typist, and in spite of the problem with spell checkers, automated bibliography editors can be expected to do their job increasingly well as proxies for *part* of the job of a human editor. We can also see that spell checkers and speech transcribers would make good tools so long as their limitations are understood—they can amplify and improve our abilities to do things.

There is, of course, another way to make mimeomorphicity acceptable higher up the tree. This is to change our forms of life. If, say, we begin to speak after the fashion of George Orwell's *1984,* we could have mechanical speaking proxies just as we now have mechanical telephone number–uttering machines. Speech transcribers and spell checkers would then do a much better job as proxies rather than tools.

Our story is about the ultimate limits of proper attribution of agency to machines. How far up the tree can we go? Our argument is simply that we cannot see how to properly extend agency to machines beyond the point in the tree where polimorphic actions begin.

How Machines Work

Doubtless, as machines develop, their potential for use as proxies creeps up the tree a bit, even if everything else we do remains the same. How much difference does the improvement in mechanism make? Previous analyses of types of machine generally talk of devices "acting." Action, as we have stressed, however, is for us a term that connotes intention, and machines do not have intentions. In our terminology, machines "behave"; machines, then, are "behavers."

Bright (1958) divided machines up into seventeen types, but for our purposes we need four:

Behavers: Behavers just do the same thing over and over again. An automatic drilling machine is an example of a behaver.

Disjunctive behavers: Disjunctive behavers do one of a set choice of things according to a predetermined list of choices. A chair-spraying robot, programmed to recognize which of a set of types of chair is currently in front of it, and to operate the corresponding program, is a disjunctive behaver.

Feedback behavers: Feedback behavers respond not to a fixed set of possibilities but to anything within a preconceived *range* of sensed stimuli. A car wash is a feedback behaver—it senses the shape of the car and adjusts the position of the rollers accordingly for any shape of car so long as it is within a preset range (and doesn't have a radio aerial or too many other loose bits). Note that the behavior of a feedback behaver is not predictable in advance; whenever a manufacturer decides to produce a new model of car, a car wash encountering the new model will follow a sequence of movement that was impossible for the car-wash designers to predict.

Learning behavers: Learning behavers take in information from their environment and their users, or both, and incorporate this in their design. Examples include plaster of Paris casts such as are used for holding broken bones in place; the cast takes in information about the shape of the leg, then sets in a shape that models the limb. A pair of good heavy leather boots is similar—they "learn" the shape of the foot—though with boots the learning process is never quite complete. In the same class are rule-inducing expert systems, which establish the "shape" of their program through comparing examples and using feedback from their "trainers," and, of course, neural nets, which carry the process further. Most rule-inducing expert systems and neural nets are much more like plaster casts than heavy boots, because they are "set" after the learning period is complete. Some expert systems (such as the crystal-growing system described in Collins [1990]), can continue to learn from their users, however, and this, no doubt, is the aim of neural net designers.

Interim Summary

The argument so far can be summed up diagrammatically (see figure 7.1). Here tools, proxies, and novelties are represented by triangles, while human action is represented by a rectangle of polimorphic actions

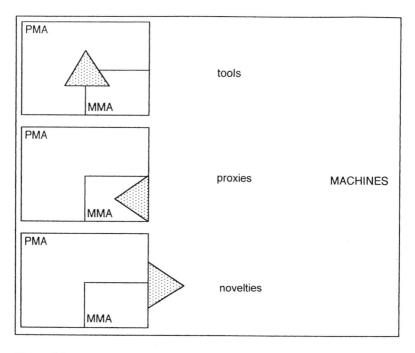

Figure 7.1
The territories of machines and actions.

enclosing a rectangle of mimeomorphic action. Tools meld into the world of polimorphic actions (though close examination from a vantage point low in the tree would reveal them to be proxies, managing the mimeomorphic elements of polimorphic actions). Novelties extend our abilities, and, thought of as tools from a high level of the tree, they amplify our abilities. (It is easy to see that a hammer can be thought of as a tool or as a novelty.) Thus in the diagram, novelties are shown extending out to the right beyond the domain of human action and into the unknown. Proxies are invading the inner rectangle and taking it over (usually to our great relief and pleasure). Proxies do better and better as they gain abilities such as learning from feedback; they push into the domain of mimeomorphic action.[13] On this diagram, the only difference between a

13. In Bright's (1958) account, people working in factories needed less and less skill as proxies invaded the whole of our territory; on our account, and the account of many of those who have carried out "studies of work," factory

canoeing machine and a bicycle-balancing machine is that the first has not yet been developed, and the second has.[14]

It may be that humans too are engaged in their own invasion. Here and there perhaps, humans are invading the territory of novelties. Through studies of diet and training regimes, athletes are getting stronger and faster, learning how to do things that once only machines could do. Perhaps, with careful use of biofeedback, abuse of drugs, and interference with our genes, we humans will one day teach ourselves how to do what only a fridge-freezer can do today; we may one day be able to freeze ice with our bare hands! But if we do, we will probably be able to do it in two ways, involving polimorphic actions, or mimeomorphic actions. Machines—at least, the ones we understand today—will still only be able to mimic mimeomorphic water freezing.

The Phylogenetic Scale of Machines

It is tempting to think that as machines begin to learn from feedback, they are approaching us in ability. Where should we put machines on the phylogenetic scale of living organisms? Around the level of apes, perhaps? Our diagram is meant to suggest that the invasion of proxies will not cross the boundary of the polimorphic actions rectangle. In part, our choice of examples was also made to prevent too optimistic a judgment. While a neural net can be thought of as "almost human" because of the way it "learns" from feedback, "works out" its own rules, and "remembers" them, it is less tempting to impute intelligence to a car wash or a pair of old boots.[15] Why is this? The answer seems to have something to do with what we count as one of the high-water marks of human ability.

---

workers, even those who attend highly automated machines, still need all the skills associated with the contents of the polimorphic actions rectangle. Bright (1958), is quoted in Braverman (1974, p. 216). This point will be discussed at greater length in the chapter on bureaucracies and mechanistic systems. We are grateful to Jamie Fleck for drawing this material to our attention.

14. And this, to reiterate a point, is why the term "situated action," which covers both canoeing and socially situated actions, does not fit neatly into our scheme.

15. Though Herbert Simon (1969) seems ready to impute intelligence to a thermostat.

Once upon a time, the ability to calculate was taken as the true stamp of cleverness. The invention of computers has done something to lower this ability in our estimation. Nevertheless, while calculation is no longer a high point, it does seem to be an essential ability for those entities to which we attribute intelligence; an old boot does not calculate.

On the other hand, a simple program such as ELIZA does its work through calculation and it must be this, in part, that makes it such a tempting candidate for charitable assessment.[16] So long as acting competently *in the flux of social life* is not taken as the quintessential mark of human ability, we will think of ourselves as complicated ELIZAs, and ELIZA will continue to look good. Thus the typology of the ways in which machines work, set out above, if it is a phylogenetic scale, has a much narrower range than first appears. If we can establish the crucial importance of social abilities, we will have shown that even the most advanced neural nets are at the level of the mollusk. We will return to this theme in the conclusion.

Indifference Matching: The Sociology of the Same

The typology of the ways in which machines work matches our typology of human mimeomorphic action. Ordinary mimeomorphic actions can be replaced by behavers, and the various kinds of disjunctive mimeomorphic actions can be replaced by disjunctive, feedback, and learning behavers. These kinds of machines have the potential to be our proxies under the appropriate circumstances. But what are these circumstances? It is a matter of "the sociology of the same."

The whole pattern of human life could be said to be a matter of what we see as the same and the way boundaries between things are shifted about. Artists, scientists, politicians, writers, and all the others who help to change our culture are all the time trying to establish new relations of similarity and difference. To return to the more mundane example discussed in an earlier chapter, what makes golfers golfers is that two 300-yard drives are seen as the same if they follow a similar flight path and land within a few feet of each other, whereas what makes dog owners

16. See Collins (1990).

dog owners is that they see those two drives as different if one hits a dog and the other does not; what makes engineers engineers is the tendency to see the two golf swings as different in terms of the scale on which engineers usually measure things. The golfer, as golfer, is indifferent to the differences seen by the engineer and the dog owner. We can happily use machines as our proxies when the envelope of our indifference to the way we execute our actions is no narrower than the envelope of variation in the behavior of the machine. It happens, then, that we can build machines that can drive golf balls with less variation than that of the best golfer—one such is known as "Iron Byron." It is a fine golf ball–driving machine. Indeed, since even the best golfers would prefer to drive with less variation than they can actually achieve, they count Iron Byron as a better driver than themselves.

There are, on the other hand, no machines that could replace golfers in the whole of the game.[17] That is because our envelopes of indifference for how the whole game is played are relatively narrow. The action "playing a game of golf" is full of structure that we care about deeply. To get to areas of indifference within which a machine or machines could fit, we have to go well down the tree to aspects of the game such as driving.

Of course, the structure within a triangle of action can be matched by a machine so long as it is a disjunctive structure—a matter of specifiable relations and functions—but the whole game of golf is not like this.

Let us explore the matter in the context of another of our standard examples. Consider the way a pocket calculator is made to fit into our form of life. Consider especially the example of 7/11x11 when the calculator gives 6.99996 as the answer. What we do when that happens is to repair the calculator's problem—we say "it really means seven," so it is as though the calculator has never done anything wrong at all. Now consider the sum "7/2x2." Most calculators will give the answer "7" to this sum, which we count as the correct answer. But suppose I happen to have a calculator that gives the answer "7." Do I "repair" the

17. We ignore the whimsy inherent in trying to replace a human golfer with a machine—that of course would destroy the point of the game as a test of human skills. We are talking here of in-principle, engineering feasibility.

calculator's answer? Does the question make sense? At this point the reader may be thinking that the copy editor has made a mistake. The reason the question does not seem to make sense is that there is nothing to repair. The answer "7" and "7" are different but not in a way that is in need of repair as far as arithmetic is concerned. We are indifferent to the difference between 7 and 7 in a way that we were not indifferent to the difference between 7 and 6.99996. Or to put it another way, our indifference to the difference between 7 and 6.99996 is an active indifference—it requires us to do something positive in the way of repairing so that the difference does not count anymore, whereas our indifference to 7 and 7 is passive.

That passivity does not have to do with the magnitude of the difference between, on the one hand, 7 and 7 and, on the other hand, 7 and 6.99996. There is no absolute magnitude to these things. It has to do with the relationship of the numbers to the form of life of arithmetic. The way we cut things up in arithmetic makes 7 and 7 "the same" while 7 and 6.99996 are different unless we do something about it. But we could imagine it otherwise. We could imagine that the difference between ordinary and bold print comes to have an arithmetical significance. In that case, the bold 7, if it was the wrong answer, would need repair in the same way as 6.99996 does now.

The importance of these examples is to show that while the theory of the shape of actions (the theory of action morphicity) is a human-centered theory, as are theories of repair or attribution, the center is in a different place. Repair or attribution theories account for every feature of a mechanism, such as a calculator, by reference to users' interactions with it. The theory of action morphicity accounts for some features of such a mechanism by reference to the interactions of users among themselves, at a point logically prior to their encounter with the mechanism. The first type of theory says that whatever the mechanism is seen to be is a matter of the way the users see it; the theory of action morphicity says that whether a mechanism will fit into a form of life without repair depends on the form of life. A mechanism may be made to fit better or worse by changing the form of life. How much repair work needs to be done is a matter of the extent to which form of life and mechanism match. They may come to match more closely if the form of life comes to contain more mimeomorphic actions. They may be either *casual mimeomorphic actions,* so that we are indifferent to more things, or *special mimeomorphic actions,* so that where machines produce what we count as constancy of outcome we are especially pleased. When machines act as proxies in replacing casual mimeomorphic actions, we like it because it saves us time and energy; when machines replace special mimeomorphic actions we like it even more because, usually, we consider that the machines do a better and more accurate job than ourselves. Machines are usually better than us at generating behaviors equivalent to special mimeomorphic actions—good machines are made that way.

There are several *sociologies of the same.* There is the sociology of how new relationships of sameness are established—this is what the sociology of scientific knowledge is about. Studies of "scientific discovery" show us developing new ranges of indifference to variation; a laser that works is "the same as" another laser that works irrespective of the multitudinous small differences of construction; a laser that does not work is "different" to one that does work even if there are no differences apparent to the eye.

Another sociology has to do with the ordinary application of the word "same" to broad classes of entities; what sort of thing do we associate with constancy. For modern Westerners, the idea that we can never step into the same river twice comes as a bit of a shock, because the scientific viewpoint, as opposed to, say, the magical, makes nature a hallmark of constancy and predictability. Machines, too, are thought of as reproducers of constancy and predictability. Detailed studies of machines, such as Kusterer (1978), which show them to vary markedly from individual model to individual model, again disturb our preconceptions. That which is human and human-sized seems to us to be variable and "rough," while that which is mechanical and small seems to us to be constant and "smooth." To us, a paradigm of smoothness is a polished metal surface— say the inside of the cylinder belonging to the engine of a modern car—but examined under the microscope it is a mountain range of jagged hills and valleys. All smoothness, all constancy, is relative in this way; it depends on perspective, and therefore all judgments of smoothness and constancy depend on the choice of scale. The sociology of the same is about the differing application of the terms constancy, smoothness, and so forth, in different forms of life. What we have tried to show is that in spite of the long-term relativity of the application of such terms, it is still possible to make mistakes in applying them. If we do not, as a society, feel indifferent to certain differences, then a machine that is indifferent to those differences will not reproduce our actions satisfactorily. To call an action mimeomorphic is to describe the area within which we feel indifferent to the behavioral instantiation of the action. Indifference and similarity are the same idea; it is indifference that allows us to induce.[18]

Summary

The analysis of machines that might be used to help us write showed how intimate and complex is the relationship between ourselves and machines, and yet how the idea that only mimeomorphic actions can be replaced by machines robustly survives examination.

We went on to typologize the role of machines into three categories— tools, proxies, and novelties. We showed how taking different perspectives alters our concept of which of these things a machine is. We showed, nevertheless, that it is still possible to make a mistake by choosing the wrong idea about a machine from a particular perspective. The idea of RAT was used to show why the nature of machines' contribution is so easily overlooked. Repair, Attribution, and all That is such a widespread facility that we use it all the time without noticing, thus causing us to anthropomorphize mechanisms. The only kind of mechanism that should be a candidate for the label "humanlike" is one that has as much facility at RAT as ourselves. We have no such devices except where mimeomorphic actions are concerned; in this respect, Iron Byron is more humanlike than ELIZA.

We then typologized machines into different types of "behavers" and discussed the phylogenetic scale of devices. This way of looking at things showed the relationship between tough boots, plaster casts, and neural

18. Rule-inducing expert systems put the cart before the horse. Enthusiasts for such expert systems believe the systems will discover the regularities in the world, whereas it is we who decide on the regularities by deciding on the things we are indifferent to. This abstract idea has quite concrete manifestations in the failure of so-called discovery programs (see, for example, Collins 1989).

nets. We used a diagram to look at the intermingling of machines and humans in another way. Finally, we showed how the idea of indifference and the idea of mimeomorphicity were related. Thus we see what humans and machines can do.

Appendix: A Robot Slave

Suppose a robot followed its owner about, mimicking everything that he or she did? If the robot was successful, showing that every action that the person did could be mimicked by a machine, would this show that every action the person did was mimeomorphic?[19]

We describe machines as "mimicking" actions rather than acting, so as to make clear that entities that do not have intentions do not act. When we say that a machine mimics an action we mean that the *consequence* of the mimicry is the same as the *result* of the action. There is, however, another use of the term "mimic." The type of robot mentioned in the query mimics the behavior, but this does not necessarily have consequences that are the same as the result of the action. This is not surprising in the case of polimorphic actions. For example, if the robot's owner greets a secretary with a cheery "hello," and the robot immediately repeats the greeting in the same tone of voice with the same gestures, this is likely to be seen as "mockery" rather than greeting. To copy the behavior associated with the action of greeting—which means having it carried out twice, not once—is not to mimic the action.[20] The same goes for *mimeomorphic* actions where a double execution does not have the same value as a single execution. Mimicry of behavior is often used as mockery by humans as well as by machines, and it matters not whether the action corresponding to the behavior is polimorphic or mimeomorphic. What we conclude is that not all copying of behavior, even in the case of mimeomorphic actions, is mimicry of the action. Nevertheless, no action can be mimicked by copying the action unless it is a mimeomorphic action.

19. This question was put to us by Olga Amsterdamska.

20. There are a number of alternative analyses possible. Perhaps a low-level action is being mimicked—e.g., "saying hello"—whereas the higher-level action—"greeting"—was not.

Now let us make the case more difficult. Going back to the polimorphic action of greeting, suppose the owner's robot, instead of following the owner around, was controlled remotely by the owner's actions. In a scenario beloved of philosophers, the robot's owner sits at home while the robot-facsimile wanders around in the world with its senses fully and instantly linked to the owner's senses via telemetry—the robot is controlled by the owner's movements—everything the owner does and says, it does and says.

Through the eyes of the robot the owner sees the secretary and cries "hello." The machine mimics the owner's behavior, but on this occasion it also has the effect of executing a greeting. On the face of it, the robot has mimicked a polimorphic action without having to be socialized first. Does the theory fall?

It does not fall, because the robot is a tool rather than a proxy. Or, to be more exact, it is a proxy only when the elements of the action are broken down into very small bits indeed. As far as the action of greeting is concerned, the robot is not doing the owner's action for the owner, merely enabling the owner to do the action better—that is, from a remote site. To think of the robot as mimicking the action of greeting is a bit like thinking of the owner's lips and mouth as mimicking the action of greeting when the owner says "hello." The owner's lips and mouth are not mimicking the action, they are helping the owner execute it. The robot is the same.

8

Organizations and Machines

Machines fit into human societies with behaviors and mimeomorphic actions. How do humans fit into machines? *Chambers English Dictionary* includes the following definition of machine: "any artificial means or contrivance: an engine: one who can do only what he is told: an organized system: a political party organization." Under "machine code or machine language," the dictionary says: "instructions for processing data, put into a form that can be directly understood by a computer." *The Oxford English Dictionary* includes among its definitions: "A combination of parts moving mechanically, as contrasted with a being having life, consciousness and will. Hence applied to a person who acts merely from habit or obedience to a rule, without intelligence, or to one whose actions have the undeviating precision and uniformity of a 'machine.'" To what extent do these definitions make sense in terms of the theory of the shape of actions?[1]

1. We know from work such as Kusterer's (1978) studies of a paper factory that technicians sometimes need to "know" machines as individuals if they are to get them to produce steady and reliable output—that is, machines are not as unvarying as the metaphor would suggest. Kusterer's and others' analyses of the nature of machines will turn out to be important as we come to look at the way humans interact with industrial machinery, but in respect of the applicability of the machine metaphor it is a detail. The kind of individual quirkiness found in machines is not the same as that found in humans. Machines might respond to the damp, to the light, to a good kicking, but they are not affected by the atmosphere of the 1960s, status disequilibrium, or loss of perks. At least, insofar as they are affected by such things it is indirectly—as a result of the responses of their human keepers. The quirkiness of machines results from "defects."

Bureaucracies, Mechanistic Systems, Microworlds

Max Weber's treatment of bureaucracy is the locus classicus of the idea of an organization as a machine.[2] Weber considered bureaucratic organization to be fair and efficient. Smith (1988), surveying various uses of the term, includes the following elements in the definition:

A bureaucracy consists of a number of "offices". . . . The tasks, authority and duties of each office are allocated by formal rules in a regular, stable and precise manner. . . . One of the most important characteristics of pure bureaucracy . . . is that the work of the office is according to rules which are applied to cases without regard to personal considerations. The bureaucrat is expected to behave with "formalistic impersonality," treating like cases alike. (pp. 1–3)

Work in industrial sociology and the sociology of organizations has revealed the weaknesses of the machine metaphor applied to organizations. For example, Alvin Gouldner (1954) showed that bureaucratic organizations were far more complex than Weber's picture—admittedly an "ideal type"—would suggest. Gouldner is very much concerned with the basis of authority in bureaucracies. He finds a contradiction in Weber's treatment between obedience to rules as a result of authority, and deference and obedience through mutual recognition by managers and workers that bureaucracy is fair and efficient. We, however, are not concerned with motivations but the technical nature of rules and the

---

Certainly, when we build machines we try to minimize quirkiness whereas, on the whole, we value individuality in humans.

Personal computers are much better examples of machinelike machines than Kusterer's paper rollers. Over a large range of operations, modern computers are not quirky. Indeed, over a large range of operations computers made by one manufacturer can stand in place of the products of other manufacturers. IBM-compatibles really are compatible. One must accept that computers are not completely reliable, and that programs cannot be proven over the full range of potential applications, and one knows that start-up procedures, shut-down procedures, and a few other features might vary from PC to PC, but to think this is the whole story is to miss something essential about computers and similar machinery. Machines are designed to be good behavers, and on the whole they are more reliable at repetition of behavior—the kind of thing that is the instantiation of mimeomorphic action in humans—than many humans are. The characterization is reasonably fair.

2. See Gerth and Mills (1948).

behaviors they prescribe. Are rules like machine codes? Does a bureaucracy run on something like a "machine language"?

Alienated Labor

On the matter of how bureaucracies and "mechanistic systems" actually run, we find a tension in the existing literature.[3] What one might call the "alienated labor" literature has been highly critical, in the political sense, of the process of automation, but it has been uncritical in its analysis of the nature of factory work, accepting too easily the mechanical metaphor. This may be because of the way that the mechanical automation of the production line, metal machining, and so forth, have been become associated with ideas about central control. This literature associates centralized bureaucratic control with the process of mechanization. Analysts such as Braverman (1974, especially chap. 9) and Noble (1984) consider that as the need for skills is taken from the factory worker by innovations such as numerically controlled machine tools, control over the machines passes from the worker to higher levels in the organization, and this bolsters centralization. Workers become "machine minders" rather than using their skills to work with machines as tools under their control. Braverman relies heavily on the work of James R. Bright for his account of the increase in automation in the factory. He quotes him as follows:

By its very definition, the truly automatic machine needs no human assistance for its normal functioning. "Patrolling" becomes the main human contribution. The "operator," if he is still there, becomes a sort of watchman, a monitor, a helper. We might think of him as a liaison man between machine and operating management.[4]

This is not an accurate account of what happens in many factories. For instance, Jones (1982, 1997) has shown that those who "tend"

---

3. "Mechanistic system" is the term used by Burns and Stalker (1961) to describe firms in which all decision making passes through the top of the hierarchy. As with a bureaucracy, roles are circumscribed and obligations are felt to the particular role or superior, rather than to the firm as a whole. We are not concerned with the efficiency of this form of organization but with the bureaucracylike formality. For our purposes, a mechanistic system is simply the industrial manifestation of a bureaucracy; an exploration of either will shed light on the other.

4. Bright (1958), quoted in Braverman (1974), p. 220.

numerically controlled machine tools need to make continual adjustments if the machine is to cope with the mistakes of the programmers and the variations it encounters in handling real rather than notional materials. Those machinists who are determined to do a good job have to master programming skills; a lot of the programming takes place on the shop floor.

But even supposing numerically controlled machine tools worked as well as they are supposed to work, the typical description of the automated factory would still be misleading. Again following Bright, Braverman stresses the eventual downward plunge of the graph representing the skill requirements of the modernizing factory. Though the skill needed to operate the first generations of complex machinery is high, as soon as automation reaches beyond a certain level, the workers need less and less education and special training. It is a short step from here to think that the remaining "unskilled" workers with their trivial competences could be replaced by yet more machines.[5]

Bureaucratic Rules and Residual Skills

We now know that the replacement of human skills by machinery is far more difficult than was once believed, even though it is undeniable that the introduction of some types of machine leads to alienation and a degradation in the market position of labor. There is a further problem for automation beyond what has already been said about the recalcitrant nature of the machines found on many production lines. The problem is that the rules that the most "unskilled" of machine minders need to follow still demand interpretation. Gouldner (1954) understood this well. He pointed out that, on the face of it, "the rules serve to narrow the subordinate's 'area of discretion.' The subordinates now have fewer options concerning what they *may* or *may not* do, and the area of 'privilege' is crowded out by the growing area of 'obligation'" (p. 163, Gouldner's stress). But he was also aware that rules do not interpret

---

5. For another study of the relationship between automation and deskilling, see Friedman (1955). Friedman argues that automation not only reduces the need for some kinds of skills but creates the need for new ones, such as the making and maintenance of complex automatic machines. (This is a forerunner of Jones's [1982, 1997] argument applied to an earlier generation of machinery.)

themselves. Thus he pointed to the existence of what he called "bureaucratic sabotage" (what we would call "working to rule"): "by the very act of conforming to the letter of the rule, its intention is 'conscientiously' violated . . . . The worker could, as it were, take any attitude toward his work that he wished, so long as he conformed to the rules. The rules did little to modify *attitudes* toward work, but were significant primarily as guidelines for *behavior*" (p. 175, Gouldner's stress).

Even Gouldner, however, has not quite grasped the generality of the Wittgensteinian (1953) point that rules do not contain the rules for the own application; otherwise he would have been less certain that a rule can prescribe behavior. As other studies of bureaucracy have shown, the appearance of the smooth functioning of rules has to be *accomplished*.[6] Therefore rule following in a normal bureaucracy is not in tension with the exercise of skill; on the contrary, the two go together—one has to have skills to make a bureaucracy work. "Working to rule," or "bureaucratic sabotage," is not overzealous obedience to rules, for it is never clear what counts as obedience outside of sets of social conventions. Likewise, bureaucratic obstructionism—the sort of thing that can be encountered by the customers of a large organization—cannot be what it is often called; it cannot be the "mindless" following of rules because in the normal way there is no such thing as the mindless following of a rule (we will come to exceptions later). We have to redefine "mindless" rule following, or bureaucratic sabotage-type "pedantic" rule following, as interpretations of rules designed to express power, or to further the interests of the organization rather than the customer, or some such. Let us illustrate the point with examples.

"Mindless Bureaucracy": The New Delhi Sheraton

One of the authors was once at the Sheraton Hotel in New Delhi standing in line for an airplane ticket to Benares. There were two lines, one for

---

6. The process is akin to what has been discovered in the sociology of scientific knowledge (SSK). Indeed, one might say that much of the last two decades of SSK has been a matter of showing how scientists, technologists, and technicians give the untidy world of the laboratory the appearance of perfectly regulated order, an order that is then said to have emerged from the preexisting orderliness of nature.

the international airline carrier, and one for the internal carrier. To get from the end of either line to the desk took about two hours. When the lady immediately in front of the author reached the desk, she asked for a ticket to London. With delight (it seemed), the clerk informed her that she was in the wrong line and would have to start all over again. The lady burst into tears, but the clerks behind the desk would do nothing for her.

What rules were the clerks obeying? One might say they were simply obeying the rules of issuing internal tickets in one place and international tickets at the other. But this would not prevent them issuing an international ticket from the appropriate station and handing it to the lady standing elsewhere. One might say that they were enforcing the rules of orderly queuing, but the lady had already stood in line for two hours; if she had joined the right line two hours previously, she would by now have reached the front of the international line. As it was, the lady had to wait in line for four hours instead of two, and could, therefore, be said to have "lost" the place she first occupied when she entered the bureau. One simply cannot say that what the clerks did was a matter of following the rules exactly, because the meaning of an "exact following" of the queuing rule is not obvious: Is it two hours queuing or four? What the clerks were doing was exploiting their power and legitimating their actions through a plausible interpretation of the rules, which they also had the power to insist was the correct interpretation. The clerks, then, were not mindlessly following rules, but skillfully interpreting them to a certain end.

"Complete Deskilling": McDonald's

What then is deskilling, and why does it still seem to take place? The answer is that it is the process of replacing esoteric with ubiquitous skills. We can see this happening in a case of what has been called "complete deskilling."

One of the most startling examples of these processes is the progress of the McDonald's fast food chain. Barbara Garson (1988) describes the workings of a branch of the firm. Garson starts by quoting a McDonald's employee as follows: "And that's what [McDonald's] is, a machine. You don't have to know how to cook, you don't have to know how to think.

There's a procedure for everything and you just follow the procedures" (p. 17).

In a branch of McDonald's the cooking of each item is timed and controlled by buzzers and beepers, the french fries are automatically controlled by a computerized probe in the vat of oil, the portions of fries are controlled by the shape of the scoop. Garson says, "By combining twentieth-century computer technology with nineteenth-century time-and-motion studies, the McDonald's corporation has broken the jobs of griddleman, waitress, cashier and even manager down into small, simple steps. Historically these have been service jobs involving a lot of flexibility and personal flair. But the corporation has systematically extracted the decision-making elements" (p. 37).

The success of these mechanisms is signified by the extraordinary staff policy of McDonald's; they don't have to care about staff turnover. Training takes fifteen minutes and full efficiency, according to McDonald's founder, is reached in half an hour. A large proportion of the training is done by the potential employee watching a video. Because training is so quick and simple, McDonald's can afford not to care about staff turnover. If someone works in McDonald's for only one day and then leaves, that is not necessarily inefficient.[7] Garson says, "They've siphoned the know-how from the employees into the programs" (p. 37).

In her book, Garson goes on to describe the reformation of the tasks of, among others, social workers, airline reservation clerks, and stockbrokers. In each case, computer monitoring and other types of surveillance, allied to the breaking down of the task into component parts, has turned what was once a highly skilled job into what seems to be a mechanical routine. Garson believes we are only a short step from the replacement of the human operatives who fill these roles by machines made out of metal and silicon rather than flesh and blood. McDonald's is only the most striking example of a more widespread phenomenon.

This picture is incorrect. Clearly something remarkable has happened at McDonald's, and clearly some human skills have been made redundant

---

7. We are not in a position to verify whether this is really true, but for the purposes of the argument, it does not matter if things are not quite so straightforward. There must be circumstances where they could be this simple.

by mechanisms, but the residual work force remains skilled, even if they sometimes look like fools.[8] Let us think about just one link in the chain—the counter clerks. Garson thinks that the counter clerks have been deskilled because they no longer have to know even the prices of the goods they sell (in fact, as she points out, they do not know them). All the clerks have to do is press keys marked with symbols representing the limited range of items that McDonald's sells—a regular hamburger, a quarter-pounder, Chicken McNuggets, small, medium, or large fries, and so forth. When the appropriately marked keys are pressed, the prices are automatically entered and added, the sum that the customer must pay appearing on the screen. But to get as far as entering the key presses, the clerk has to engage in a enormously skilled conversational interaction with the customer. The clerk has to understand what the customer wants. There is no existing computer that could understand the variety of accents and modes of expression that customers currently use in placing their orders at McDonald's. Every clerk has to have undergone the extraordinary long and difficult process of training called socialization, compared to which any kind of on-the-job training, however complex, is a mere bagatelle. None of this is to say that the routine practice of these extraordinary skills is not alienating.

Why is it so easy to think of the McDonald's labor force as unskilled? What is it about the labor force that makes it possible for McDonald's to have such a cavalier labor turnover policy? It is that the remaining skills of the counter clerks are ubiquitous; almost everybody has them. The clerks have the skills of Repair, Attribution, and all That which we discussed in chapter 7 under the heading of RAT. This means that they can take anyone off the street and expect them to exercise that level of skill with hardly any training. But to mistake this for no skill—and to conclude that it is but a short step to the replacement of the counter clerks by machines—is to make a serious mistake.

But, one might say, the counter clerks could be replaced by mechanisms as they are in the case of automatic food-vending machines. Suppose

8. The typical American franchise operative looks like a fool when confronted with a problem that is not covered in the rule book. One of the authors has had extraordinarily difficult encounters with American banks whose operatives seem incapable of dealing with the special needs of a foreign customer.

McDonald's turned the cash registers round so that the customers could press the symbols themselves without the conversational intercession of the clerks. We have still not deskilled the task, it is just that we have transferred the responsibility of exercising the skills to the customers. Once again, because the required skill is ubiquitous, we could reasonably expect this to work.[9]

In certain countries the process of transference of skills from the clerk to the customer has already been accomplished via a different mechanism. For example, in parts of Germany branches of McDonald's are staffed almost exclusively by non-German speakers. It is the responsibility of the customer entering such an establishment to make him- or herself understood. This they generally do by pointing to items on the large menu displayed behind the counter.

The advantage of looking carefully at what is going on in the case of McDonald's is that we can see how different are the cases Garson dealt with, despite her lumping them together. For example, the second case she deals with is airline reservation clerks. She shows how the area of discretion of the clerks has been reduced; each of their booking interactions with customers is broken down into stages: "opening," "sales pitch," "probe," and "close." And yet the amount of specialized skill that the booking clerks still require is large compared to the McDonald's case. While the booking clerks are not *absolutely* more skilled, the esoteric nature of what they have to know makes it impossible to simply "turn the consoles round" in the way that McDonald's cash registers could be turned, or to ask the passengers to take on the responsibility.

A Note on Science

Something of the same analysis that applies to McDonald's applies to science. What one might call "the canonical model of science," the model that is enshrined both in commonsense accounts of scientific procedure and in at least some philosophical analyses, treats science as a bureau-

9. Presumably there are other reasons that stop McDonald's introducing such a policy: a cash register cannot offer that small moment of human contact that McDonald's customers expect! Imagine a McDonald's equipped with automated

cratic mechanism. Science works when the rules are followed by scientists without bias or favor. Since nature is unambiguous (if reticent) about revealing her secrets, adherence to a bureaucratic algorithm, which includes prescriptions for the conduct of experiments as well as for interpersonal behavior, will separate the true face of nature from a false image.[10] It could be said that the contribution of the sociology of scientific knowledge has been to show that a bureaucratic algorithm is no more workable in science than it is in any industrial organization.[11]

The canonical, bureaucratic model remains highly pervasive, even among scientists themselves. It acts as a kind of founding myth, but a myth that can lead to disappointment and misdirected effort. For example, in the early 1970s many scientists were trying to build a new kind of laser—the Transversely Excited Atmospheric Pressure Carbon Dioxide laser, or TEA laser. Laser builders always started by trying to follow a set of written instructions, such as were available in the literature, as closely as possible. They always failed. But the failure always came as a surprise and a disappointment.[12] We could say that the laser scientists were informed by the idea of science as a set of mimeomorphic actions; identical physical movements prescribed by rules should give rise to identical degrees of success. In this case the illusion could not be maintained because the culture of TEA laser building was not sufficiently well distributed to allow for appropriate interpretation of the instructions. The "output" of the written articles could not be sufficiently well repaired by the scientists. Only after interacting with colleagues—telephoning, watching, imitating, and experimenting—did they learn enough of the culture to do their experiments successfully. It turns out that the world of science, which is presented as quintessentially a domain of

---

tills and change machines and staffed by no one but security guards; it would not be a welcoming place.

10. The conventional view accepts that inspirational genius may be required in the arena of discovery, but the bureaucratic algorithm still applies in the arena of justification; it is said to be the method of justification that makes science what it is.

11. There is a large literature on the sociology of scientific knowledge. A simple introduction is Collins and Pinch (1993).

12. See Collins (1974); Collins and Harrison (1975).

mimeomorphic actions, is heavily dependent on the ability to act polimorphically.

The polimorphic aspect of science has been extraordinarily well hidden. Much of the myth of science is supported by what one might call in our terminology, RAT-filled history. That is to say, the untidy elements of passages of scientific research as they were conducted by scientists have been repaired by popularizing historians so that they can attribute mimeomorphicity to the process. Computer scientists, taken in by the myth, have gone so far as to try to build computers that make scientific discoveries; the computer scientists have even managed to convince themselves that the programs work.[13]

The sociological analysis of science is rather like the sociological analysis of work; what were once thought to be factories full of humans-turned-machines have turned out to be full of men and women adjusting and repairing their actions to fit a disordered world of machinery within rich social contexts. Science, once thought to be a domain of humans-turned-apparatus, has turned out to be made of men and women acting like men and women everywhere, though often mistaking what they are doing for the workings of some giant computer program. There are some bits of science that are mimeomorphic; in any field of science the ratio of mimeomorphic to polimorphic actions probably increases slightly as controversies settle into consensus, but the domain of mimeomorphic actions remains small even in the most stabilized sciences.

Technicians

It has been argued that the role of technicians in the scientific laboratory is to do the RAT that enables scientists to carry on as though in a bureaucratically ordered world (Barley and Bechky 1994). In fact the scientific laboratory does not partition neatly into scientists on the one hand and technicians on other; everyone is engaged in the continual making of order out of disorder. There is, however, a need for a general analysis of the role of "technician"—widely construed—in science and other places. If we take a technician to be one who works with machines

13. See Langley et al. (1987); Collins (1989, 1990).

and in machines, then we can see that there is a set of generic roles that could be adopted. There are technicians who, using their RAT skills to effect, make bits of the ordinary world function like smooth running machines for themselves and the rest of us—they digitize the undigitized output of the world so that it will fit with other machines. The McDonald's counter clerks fulfill this role—they take the messy comments of the customers and turn them into the digital inputs needed by the cash registers.

The complementary kind of technician is one who tends machines with an output that is too awkward and rigidly digital to fit with the rest of the world, and using the same kind of skills as before, undigitizes the output so that it fits back into the world. Any user of a pocket calculator is such a technician.

A third kind of "technician" is one who tends a bureaucracy that has the capacity to deal with the world but presents it as much more rigidly machinelike than it is. The widespread idea of the machine makes this role a possibility—too many people are ready to accept that "the machine will not allow them to do this or that." The counter clerks at the New Delhi Sheraton were technicians of this sort.

The Bureaucratic Room

Having shown that there is normally no such thing as "mindless rule following," we now want to reinstate the notion. The idea of mindless rule following does have applications, even if they are not what they are generally taken to be. What could mindless rule following be? One way to think about this is to imagine a situation in which the person following the rules could *not* use his or her mind because they did not understand the instructions they were following. John Searle's (1980) idea of the "Chinese Room" comes in quite handy in creating such a scenario. The "Chinese Room" contains someone who does not speak Chinese, but is supplied with a set of look-up tables in which sets of Chinese symbols correspond to other sets of Chinese symbols. Chinese speakers pass written questions or comments into the room; these appear to the person in the room as meaningless symbols. The person matches these with the squiggles in the "left" column of the table, copies out the corresponding squiggles on the "right," and returns them. The corresponding squiggles, unknown to the person in the room, are reasonable conversational responses to the original conversational turns. We would argue, against Searle, that this arrangement could not reproduce normal written Chinese conversation,[14] but it will serve to help us understand what is meant by following instructions without interpretation. In what one might call an "ideal bureaucracy," a "Chinese" room (in which the "conversation" was conducted in whatever was the appropriate language) could serve as a link in a chain of command. Every appropriate response or order to every conceivable query or problem would have to be worked out in advance and inscribed in the book of rules;[15] impersonality is, of course, guaranteed since the bureaucrat could not know how to respond in such a way as to show favoritism. Let's call such an arrangement a "bureaucratic room."

It is worth noting that the person in a bureaucratic room *could* be replaced by a machine, which would need to do no more than match one well-defined pattern with another, or by a well-trained animal such as a pigeon which could, perhaps, peck at the relevant entries. Likewise the job could be done by a trained human who had no idea what part they were playing in the overall bureaucratic, or even linguistic, scheme of things; that is, the human could be trained in the same way as a pigeon or other animal. For something that approaches a real example, think of the McDonald's branches staffed by nonnative speakers. By contrasting them with the bureaucratic room, it is easy to see that most bureaucratic or other "formal" systems rest on the culture-bound skills of the humans within them—the skills that enable the humans to understand the instructions. In the normal way, the appearance of formality is an artifice. A similar analysis applies to mechanistic systems.

Microworlds

It is worth exploring the idea of perfect rule following from the other end too; consider the idea of a "microworld." The initial notion of a

14. For this argument, see, for example, Collins (1990, 1996). We might say that the Chinese Room would only produce Chinese whispers.

15. It is, of course, more complicated than this. Computers do not have all their responses worked out in advance, but in principle they could. It would be nice

microworld can be taken from Terry Winograd's critical discussion of his own artificial intelligence program "SHRDLU."[16] SHRDLU is a program that encapsulates an imaginary world of colored blocks of different shapes. SHRDLU appeared to be able to converse sensibly about this world; it could be instructed to grasp the blocks, put them on top of each other, and so forth, and then answer questions in ordinary English about their dispositions.

In the early 1970s the performance of SHRDLU seemed to represent a breakthrough in artificial intelligence but the program's success is due, in spite of appearances, to its working within a world in which the range of meanings for terms is circumscribed—a microworld. Take the word "pyramid": Insofar as this word could be said to mean anything within SHRDLU, it means a pyramid-shaped colored block. It cannot mean what "pyramid" means in Egypt, for it would make no sense to try to "grasp" such a pyramid. As artificial intelligence researchers continually rediscover, an approach that is successful within a microworld cannot be extended to encompass the complexity, variability, and creativity of the real world.

In the language of the theory of the shape of actions, one would say that artificial microworlds reproduce behavior that is the counterpart of mimeomorphic actions but not of polimorphic actions. One may usefully extend the term to cover its human counterparts as well. Thus SHRDLU is a microworld like other self-contained computer games and indeed all computer programs. Ideal bureaucracies, as we have discussed them above, are microworlds, too. Other kinds of reliable machine are also microworlds. This leads us to the following definition:

A microworld is any combination of humans and machines that can operate successfully in response to an exhaustible set of bits of information without needing the interpretative skills, however ubiquitous, that come with socialization.

According to this account, microworlds are, singly or in combination, properly functioning programs, machines, natural events, or ideal bu-

---

for program provers if the potentially exhaustibility of computer programs were not rendered impractible for testing purposes by the combinatorial explosion.

16. See Winograd and Flores (1986).

reaucracies. Where humans take part in a microworld, their actions will be mimeomorphic actions or mere reflex behavior (such as that of the musketman to be described below).[17]

Drill: Anticipatory Drill, Exercise Drill, Training

Military drill is a particularly striking example of the idea of a bureaucratic room or microworld that contains humans. Certain kinds of military drill put the ideal of the organization as mechanism into practice almost without loss.

By "drill" we mean "extended repetitions of a behavioral routine." There are two kinds of drill which, as far as we can see, have not previously been distinguished: "anticipatory drill" and "exercise drill." Anticipatory drill is repetitive rehearsal of a piece of behavior prior to and away from the scene of its intended use; the behaviors mastered

17. The science of time and motion study in industrial settings, which was associated with ideas of "scientific management," attempts to break down workers' movements into basic atoms. One scheme, named after the pioneering work of the Gilbreths (1914), used a classification made up of "therbligs" (Gilbreth spelled backward). A therblig was a movement like "grasp," "bend," "release load," and so forth. A task was broken down into a sequence of these elementary movements. Study of human movement discovered the standard time required for a human to execute each type of elementary movement, and thus the time taken for any new job made up of the basic elements could be calculated. (This explanation is taken from Braverman [1974, chap. 8], who relies heavily on Nadler [1963, pp. 298–308].)

In some ways the idea of mimeomorphicity harks back to the early modernist tendency to think of what humans do as pieces of behavior. (A useful history of this kind of approach to the study of human behavior is found in Rabinbach [1990]). The therblig is a unit of behavior that allows an action to be described in rather the same way as we talk of actions being described by the space-time coordinates of their corresponding behaviors. The small trouble with therbligs per se is that they do not seem to be atomic movements. Thus the elemental movements of a seamstress, or a watchmaker, or a scientist peering down a microscope, do not seem to be describable within the therblig scheme. The big trouble with the idea is that any scheme of this sort applies only to mimeomorphic actions. It does not make sense to describe a polimorphic action in terms of its behavioral elements. To repeat the behaviors associated with a polimorphic action is to fail to execute the action. One might think of the failure of "scientific management" as turning on the confusion between the two types of action, only one of which can be sensibly described in terms of behavioral atoms.

during an anticipatory drill are designed to be used "in anger" only later.[18] Exercise drill, on the other hand, is extended repetition of a behavioral routine intended, as with most other kinds of training, practice, rehearsal, and so forth, to enhance abilities, fitnesses, or propensities the exact behavioral application of which has not been prespecified.[19]

It is tempting to suggest that that anticipatory drill is to general training, practice, rehearsal, and so on as mimeomorphic action is to polimorphic action, but only the first part of the equivalence stands up to scrutiny. It is true that anticipatory drill is designed to improve the capacity to carry out mimeomorphic actions *or their behavioral equivalent* (see below), and is only indirectly useful (and sometimes dysfunctional), in enhancing the capacity for polimorphic actions. On the other hand, one may use exercise drills, or otherwise practice or train for an action that has reference to society, or has no reference to society at all; in the latter case the "poli" element of "polimorphic" has no bearing. Thus practice and training of every kind except anticipatory drill may

18. There does not seem to be a neat civilian equivalent of this military distinction between use in practice and use "in anger." There is the distinction in sport between practicing and competition, in the theater between rehearsal and live performance, and in the professions between training and practice (an unfortunate term), but we often fall back on the military metaphor.

19. Here is an example of exercise drill taken from a military source—the *Army Trainer* (1988–1991).

WARM UP

1. Side straddle hop	20 reps
2. Neck & shoulder stretch	10 secs
3. Tricep stretch	10 secs
4. Upper back stretch	10 secs
5. Run in place	30 secs
6. Hamstring stretch	10 secs
7. Groin stretch	10 secs
8. Thigh stretch	10 secs
9. Stomach stretch	10 secs

EXERCISES (WITH PARTNER)

1. Diamond push-ups (feet elevated)	20 secs/20 secs rest
2. Push-ups (feet elevated)	20 secs/20 secs rest
3. Wide arm push-ups (feet elevated)	20 secs/20 secs rest

Switch soldiers and repeat 1–3

These numbered exercises continue through another 27 stages.

improve one's capacity to carry out either mimeomorphic or polimorphic actions.

The Story of Military Drill

As we explained in our chapter on interaction, military drill is not a fixed thing, so before launching our analysis we will fill in some context. Anticipatory drill was important in antiquity when armies fought each other in coordinated formations. During medieval times, however, when many battles consisted of duellike encounters between mounted knights, the importance of anticipatory drill diminished to vanishing point—which is not to say that other kinds of practice and training were unimportant. Anticipatory drill returned, and saw its heyday, in the sixteenth and seventeenth centuries.[20] Sixteenth- and seventeenth-century warfare—based on pike and musket—demanded that soldiers remain in a closed formation. On the one hand, the eighteen-foot-long pike was a clumsy weapon against a more lightly armed opponent, but forceful when used by a disciplined group of pikemen that marched in step with one another.[21] On the other hand, the musket was difficult to handle and reliable only at close range. Drill was important for learning how to load the musket safely and correctly, for training to shoot at the enemy rather than one's own comrades, and for firing only when ordered to do so by one's superior officer.[22] Accordingly, the sixteenth and seventeenth centuries witnessed the publication of a great number of drillbooks, which we will discuss below.

As we move from the seventeenth to the twentieth century, marching drill still exists, but it has lost its immediate military usefulness on the battlefield.[23] Soldiers no longer march onto the battlefield in formations;

20. See, for example, van Creveld (1989, p. 93); Keegan, Holmes, and Gau (1985, p. 56).

21. van Creveld (1989, p. 91).

22. van Creveld (1989, pp. 92–93).

23. Janowitz (1960, p. 51). Here is an example of marching drill taken from a training manual "by two Officers of the Dorsetshire Regiment," published in 1914. The following is their "squad drill" (Anonymous 1914, pp. 4–7):

1. FIRST POSITION OF THE SOLDIER.
Instructor illustrates, then places the recruit correctly. Recruit's peculiarities as to position to be at once noticed, and attended to.

firearms have become much too powerful and precise to make such strategy intelligible. Marching drill has changed from an anticipatory drill

---

2. ATTENTION.

Must stand square in the ranks. Correct angle of feet—45 degrees. (Faults: Small of back unduly hollowed. Abdomen protruding. Head poking forward. Strained position.) Body well forward on the feet. Hands hang easily, knuckles outwards, thumbs to the front and touching trouser seam. Fingers lightly closed.

3. STAND AT EASE.

Feet sufficiently apart. Easy position. Dressing maintained. Men perfectly still till "Stand easy" given. Slouching attituded not permitted. "Stand-easy," always given as a command.

4. DRESSING A SQUAD WITH INTERVALS.

Dress man by man commencing from the directing flank. Extend arm to get interval. Body square. Head to move sharply.

5. TURNING BY NUMBERS.

Right and left. Chest lifted and head erect. Rear leg straight. No unnecessary stamping. Keep hands still.

6. TURNING ABOUT.

Recruit to be square to his front before closing his rear foot.

7. INCLINING TO THE RIGHT AND LEFT.

Exactly 1/2 right and 1/2 left.

8. SALUTING.

All commissioned officers (whether in or out of uniform) of H.M. Naval and Military Forces must be saluted. When on bicycle salute by turning the head smartly. When passing troops salute the C.O. and march to attention past the others. Point out who should be saluted. Disengaged arm to be steady. Recruit to look straight into the officers' eyes. Point out important bearing it has on his Battalion's credit. Hand must not cover face, finger tips should touch peak of cap just about where it joins the brim.

9. LENGTH OF PACE IN MARCHING.

The drum to be used:

Slow and quick time	. . .	30 inches
Stepping out	. . .	33 inches
Double time	. . .	40 inches
Stepping short	. . .	21 inches
Side pace	. . .	14 inches
To clear of cover another	. . .	27 inches

10. CADENCE.

Slow time	. . .	74 paces in a minute.
Quick time	. . .	120 paces in a minute = 100 yds.
Quick time	. . .	140 paces in a minute—first week's recruit training.
Double time	. . .	180 paces in a minute = 200 yds.

to an exercise drill, the residual purpose of which is training for fitness, for propensities such as obedience, and for instilling a sense of group membership. As one military sociologist observed: "Ritualism is in part a defense against anxiety."[24]

Army training manuals and magazines of more recent times emphasize that soldiers must be taught to make independent decisions on the battlefield. As one author for the glossy *Army Trainer* journal—published quarterly by the U.S. Army Training Support Center—wrote in 1991:

> Subordinate elements must learn . . . using their own judgement. . . . Every soldier must be trained to take initiatives and be rewarded for doing so. . . . Leading units in battle is not like manipulating chess pieces on a board. Instead of trying to build company or battalion "machines" that we can control in battle (which is impossible), we must focus on the more feasible and rewarding goal of building real American-style combat teams. Such teams—composed of independent, confident, thinking individuals, disciplined and well-schooled in battle judgement—can get the job done even when the boss is "out to lunch." (Noyes 1991, p. 9)

Nowadays the emphasis is on the soldier as someone who can make decisions for her- or himself, and "precision in the execution of movement both in the field and in combat [is] . . . relaxed" (Janowitz 1960, p. 39). The soldier is expected to adjust flexibly to changing circumstances.

This has not obviated the need for exercise drills, but anticipatory drills are now used less to rehearse detailed battlefield maneuvers and more

---

Use 128 per minute for drill purposes, and give short occasional burst up to 140. On the line of march, 120.

11. POSITION IN MARCHING.

March straight. Understand marching on points. Arm to swing freely, no swinging across the body, no bending at elbows, hands to go as high as waistbelt. In slow time arms kept steady by side. Feet carried straight to the front, not drawn back. Don't let the men look down.

24. "Boot camp" regimes and "square bashing" still continue, though it is hard for soldiers to understand why now that the anticipatory purpose has been lost. Many American soldiers of World War II complained that the drill was quite irrelevant to their fighting task (Stouffer 1949, pp. 76–79). Of course, we may be wrong; perhaps these routines persist not because of their exercise function but because of tradition and the self-recruitment of martinets to the role of drill sergeant.

for specified elements of a soldier's activities lower down the action tree. Soldiers still need drills such as weapons training so that they can strip and reassemble a jammed weapon, without panic, in terrifying conditions. As one "field manual" of the U.S. army writes: "Training drills provide a unit with practical and efficient methods to facilitate and integrate individual and collective training. They consist of standardized techniques and procedures, and the methods by which they are trained. Some drills, such as battle drills, must be capable of instinctive and spontaneous execution because of their importance in battle. These drills will be few in number" (Anonymous 1982, p. 7). Interestingly enough, in the three volumes of the *Army Trainer* (1988–1991), the only detailed "drill" schedule was the "physical fitness card" (Turregano and Walsh 1990, pp. 30–31), an extract from which is given in note 1.

The Heyday of Drill

Let us now return to the drillbooks of the sixteenth and seventeenth centuries.[25] They reveal a treatment of the soldier's actions in battle as machinelike or mimeomorphic.

Typically, the drillbooks of this era consisted of three main parts: a first part that described the bodily postures of the soldier and the proper handling of his weapon; a second part that defined formations; and a third part that laid down the movements of such formations. Some manuals also contained advice to the general on how to conduct a war, on how to set up camp, and on other like matters. We will present the material in the reverse order, starting with less well specified instructions and working down to the particulars.

Only in the case of the commander do the drillbooks mention the need for "knowledge, & iudgement in martial affaires."

first, that he consider the maner of the warre, the qualities of the countrey, and people, against whom he is to fight, that he may chose, and weapon his souldiers, apoint & order his bandes & army accordinglye, as for example, in plaine & open countryes, the more shott & horsemen may auaile, especiallie if there bee store of forage with all, and for Incursion the more light horse, & less cariages be necessarie, the reason is plaine, for that they are to shift from place to place,

25. Procter (1578); Barret (1598); Davies (1619); Kellie (1627); Achesome and Amsterdam Norwood (1629); Cruso (1632).

spedily to annoye thenemie here and there, whereunto in the plaine fieldes they haue scope at will, Captaynes also haue ben skilfull to trayne souldiers, to practyse them in exercyses apt and auaylable for the warres, by excellent & fitt meanes, to plant & graft in them courage. And further, especiall regard must be had of the state & scituation of the countrey, waies, & grounds, for the saufe passinge conductinge and setling of his armie or campe, for chosing the field or place for battaile, that he leade not his armie into any trappes, ambushes or streightes. (Procter 1578, bk. 1, fol. 4)

The same author stressed that "all bee it, that there can not been rules appointed, or prescribed to direct al the doinges & affaires of warre" (bk. 1, fol. 23), but this openness of context concerned only the commander—"the generall" or "captaine"—not the soldier on the frontline. In the light of this thinking about battle and war, it is not surprising that officers below the general were regarded as no more than amplifiers for the general's voice: "The Company standing right in their files and rankes . . . vnto which the Captaine hath an eye in the front, and the Lieutenant in the Reare, and the Sargeants in the flanks; the Sargeants hauing an eare to the Captaine are ready to inform the company what he commands" (Davies 1619, p. 150).

It may appear, then, that once we reach below the level of general in the armies of those times, we have no need for anything but mimeomorphic actions. Our analysis of other bureaucracies and mechanistic systems should make us wary, however. As with McDonald's we should expect to find that the "amplifiers" of the general's voice are doing more than merely amplifying—they will be interpreting. Likewise, the soldier of the line will be spending some time interpreting, too. If the order comes to feed, it is probable that the exact way of getting food has not been specified; if that were not the case, the peoples of the time would have had less fear of the armies that crossed their lands.

As we get to the ranks we do, however, find a degree of specification that first depends on ubiquitous skills but eventually seems designed to substitute for them. Definitions were given for the various motions of the whole formation, motions like "Faceing" ("a Motion transferring the Souldiers to face to the Flanke or the Reare of the Battell"), "Doubling" ("a Motion of a part of the Battell . . . whereby either the length or the deipth is augmented"), "Countermarch" ("a Motion of the whole Battell whereby the Front is brought in place of the Reare, or one Flanke in place of the other"), "Closing and Opening" ("Closing, is a drawing of the Battell to a lesse distance. Opening is an extending of it to a greater distance then it had before"), and "Conversion or Wheeling" ("a Motion of the whole Battell towards the Flankes or Reare, changing the ground") (Kellie 1627, pp. 28–93). Here the authors described both the bodily movements of the individual soldier and the resulting movement of the entire formation.

Likewise, drillmasters went to great length to define the proper distances between the soldiers in formation. For instance, Davies distinguished between two distances (1619, p. 139):

In exercising the motions there are two distances to be kept. The first is when euery one is distant from his fellow 6 foote square: that is, in File and Ranke 6 foote. The second is when euery soldier is 3 foote distant one from another, as well in File as in Ranke: And in respect the measure of such distances cannot alwaies be taken euenly by the racke of the eye; the distance of 6 foote betweene the files is measured, when the soldiers stretching out their armes, doe touch one anothers hands: and betwixt the Rankes, when that the ends of their pikes come very neere to the hams of them that march before them: And the distance of 3 foot betwixt the Files is when their elbowes touch one another: and betwixt their Rankes when they come to touch the ends of one anothers Rapiers or swords.

Often, the drill books also gave more detailed advice on how the weapon ought to be held and carried. The flavor is given in this long extract from Davies (1619, pp. 75–77):

Those that are appointed to carie Pikes . . . must likewise be aduertised which march in the formost rankes, if they be vpon the right side, to hold their Pikes continually in marching in the right hand, and vpon the right shoulder without ever changing it: and so likewise being vpon the left of the ranke, to hold it alwaies vpon the left shoulder: those that be in the midst of the rankes haue libertie to vse that side that is best for their commoditie, either vpon the right or left hand, and to moue their Pikes from shoulder to shoulder at their choice and pleasure: it is true that the iust carrying of the Pike of those that march in the midst of the rankes, is to hold it vpon the left shoulder, and to carie their right hand behind vpon their dagger, or vpon their side, and so generally all, as well they that be in the midst, as those that be in the head of the rankes are to obserue this order, to carie that hand which is at libertie behinde them, or vpon their sides. Let him march then with a good grace, holding vp his head gallantly, his pace full of grauitie and state, and such as is fit for his person, and let his body bee straight and as much vpright as is possible, and that which most imports, is that they haue alwaies their eies vpon their companions which are in ranke with them, and before them going iust one with the other, and keeping perfit distance without committing error is the least pace or step, and euery pace and motion with one accord and consent, they ought to make at one instant time. And in this sort all the rankes entirely are to go, sometimes softly, sometimes fast, according to the stroke of the drumme. The heele and tippe of their pikes would bee equally holden, both of length and height, as neere as is possible, to auiode that they fall not out to be by bearing them otherwise, like vnto organ-pipes, some long, some short. The measure and porportion thereof, to hold the heele of the Pike is this: It is necessarie for him to haue an eye to the ranke that doth march before him, and so carie the Butt-end or heele of his pike, that is may bee iust ouer against the ioynt of the hamme of the souldier, that in march shall be straight before him: and so euery one from hand to hand must obserue the proportion of that height, that is right behind von the ioynt of the knee, for by doing so they cannot commit error, carying in their march that legge that is vnder that arme that sustaines and caries the Pike of iust and euen porportion, by mouing their pace right vnder the staffe of the Pike, going in their march, as I haue said before, iust and euen, with a gallant and stately, and sumptuous space.

Finally we get to the actual manipulation of the weapon in battle. Kellie (1627, pp. 22–23) distinguished between sixteen "postures . . . when the Picke-men should use, either standing or marching," Achesome (1629, pp. 6–7) distinguished forty postures for the "musquet" man, and Cruso (1632) twenty-four positions for the cavalryman. For example, Achesome's musket positions were as follows:

1. Sinke your Musquet.
2. Handell your Musquet with your right hand.
3. Unsholder your Musquet and hold her vp.
4. Fall backe with your right leg and hand.
5. Bring your rest to your Musquet.
6. Ioyne both in your left hand.
7. Hold your Musquet mouth over your leaders right shoulder.
8. Open your pan with right finger and thumb.
9. Take your pryming wyre and clense your touchholt.
10. Blow your pan.
11. Merse with powder.
12. Close your pan.
13. Grip the but-end of your Musquet and rest with your right hand and shake off the loose powder.
14. Bring about your Musquet to your left syde.
15. Discharge your measure into into your barrell.
16. Draw foorth your scrow or ramming sticke with the middle finger and thumb of the right hand.
17. Shorten the same at your right pappe within a handfull.
18. Ram in your powder, furring, and bullet.
19. Draw foorth your scrow and shorten it as before.

20. Put vp your scrow in its place.

21. Recover your Musquet and hold it vp with your left hand.

22. Take it bee the butt hard at the pan and shoulder it.

23. Your rest being in your left hand with your thumb vpon it aboue the butt.

Discharge.

24. Sinke your Musquet.

25. Handell your Musquet.

26. Vnshoulder your Musquet.

27. Hold up your Musquet.

28. Bring your rest to your Muquet.

29. Ioyne both in your left hand.

30. Take foorth your match with the finger and thumb of the right hand.

31. Blow your match vnder your right arme.

32. Cocke your match.

33. Try your match to pan.

34. Guard your pan with the first two fingers of the right hand and the thumb at the backe of the pan.

35. Blow your match againe.

36. Take off your pan.

37. Present your Musquet vpon your rest, your left foote being at the rest vpon the ground.

38. Give fire.

39. Fall of either be the right or left hand, as the Command is given.

40. In going off take foorth your match, and returne it in your left hand againe, betwixt your little finger and middle finger, or in both, having two ends lighted.

All these movements, we may be sure, were rehearsed endlessly in anticipatory drills, and we can make some guesses about the effect of this training by extending backward from what we see of military drill today. First, there is the matter of efficiency. A group of pikemen or musketmen must work as a team if they are to be effective. A break in the line of pikes allows the cavalry through, and once the flanks are exposed the whole formation and each individual within it can be destroyed. A formation of muskets must each take their turn to fire and reload if the rhythm is not to allow the enemy to advance during any extended lulls between haphazard volleys. Volley fire is important because of the inaccuracy of the musket. Single shots will have no discernible effect on the enemy, while a volley will cause enough men and horses to fall so as to still the enemy's progress. Anticipatory drill ensures the rhythm of the formation and the efficiency of each musketman.

But perhaps more important than this is the ability of the soldier to work in conditions of the utmost terror.[26] Sociological studies of the performance of American soldiers in World War II suggested that they were ready to die because of their loyalty to fellow members of close-knit platoons; they would die for their "buddies," if not for an idea or for fear of punishment.[27] In World War I, on the other hand, soldiers went to their deaths because their exercise drills and other training had instilled obedience and (perhaps) because they knew they would be shot for cowardice if they did not advance.

But why, over the centuries has the musketman and his equivalent not run from fire? Consider the musketman's job. He must keep his place, ignoring the screams of the wounded and terrorized, stand, load, kneel, aim, fire, stand, load, kneel, aim, fire, over and over again, amid the whine and thwack of missiles splitting the air and felling his comrades. Perhaps the idea of the bureaucratic room comes to our rescue and explains what military commanders have in mind. Could the idea be that enough anticipatory drill so reduces the need for interpretation of orders that the soldier becomes merely a machine, no longer *acting* either poli-morphically or mimeomorphically but merely *behaving* in response to commands—the machine code? We do not know how commands to pikemen and musketmen were actually delivered, but it would be no surprise if they were like the modern drill sergeant's tortured syllables: not words to be understood but digitized sound symbols; not demands for obedience in the face of fear but issued as stimuli intended to elicit responses without interpretation. If this is true, then the musket forma-tion was meant to become the most ideal of ideal bureaucracies—a mechanism made of humans who had turned themselves into entities as mechanical as the muskets themselves. The mechanism is controlled by vibrations in the air emitted by the vocal chords of the sergeant; it triggers vibrations of bones in the ears of the soldiers, which activate chemical and electrical messageways, which activate numerous joints and muscles in a fixed order including the contraction of a muscle in the finger, which

26. The next section is indebted to treatments such as those of Keegan (1976, 1993) and De Landa (1991).

27. Janowitz (1960).

causes the movement of a metal "trigger," which causes fire to be put to powder and a musket ball to be projected. This is not a metaphor that can mislead as we are misled when we talk of a political machine or a bureaucratic machine. Here the components really were meant to be replaced with mechanical parts without loss of efficiency; the very inaccuracy of the musket ensured its unconcern with context. And, of course, it would not be long before the formation of musketmen was replaced with the equally undiscriminating machine gun.

Conclusion

We have looked at the notion of organizations as machines and the way that humans fit into them. We have found that the metaphor is often misleading because, just as in our analysis of actions, too idealized an analysis misses details that turn out to be crucial. To partition organizations properly into their types—those that rest upon the skilled interpretation of rules, and those that are more like ideal bureaucracies or microworlds—one has to understand the detail. The Weberian notion of bureaucracy, the mechanistic model of the factory, and the idea of "alienated labor" all work at too high a level of analysis. Ubiquitous, polimorphic skills nearly always continue to be needed even when specially trained "craft" skills have been eliminated by machinery. We have no argument with that part of the labor process debate that suggests that automation leads to the degradation of the market position of labor, but we say that the alienation and the degradation of the market position comes with a shift from esoteric to ubiquitous skills, not with the elimination of skills. The literature does not distinguish between alienated polimorphic actions and behavioral uniformity or indifference. It is the distinction between actions and behaviors, not the distinction between routine and imaginative work, that is important if the process of automation is to be understood. Only when we move to special cases of organizations that run entirely on mimeomorphic actions, or move still further to arrangements such as the musket formation, in which even mimeomorphic *actions* have been eliminated, do we begin to understand what a "human machine" means.

9

The Automation of Air Pumps

The way that technical skills, scientific closure, the building of technical devices, the automation of instruments, and the spread of scientific ideas fit together has been misunderstood. We need to understand, via the theory of morphicity, how the skills needed to operate devices change as the devices develop. We take as our example the development of vacuum pumps.

Operating an air pump today is different from operating an air pump in the time of Robert Boyle and Thomas Hobbes. We would expect that Boyle, or more particularly Boyle's assistants, would need to be more noticeably inventive and skillful than those who operate air pumps nowadays; we would expect modern air pump use to be less invested with doubts, less surrounded with the need to explore and establish what is going on, more typified by routines, and less obviously beset with the problem of "tacit knowledge." We decided to find out what it was like to create a vacuum using a modern pump, and to record the experience. We would compare this with Boyle's experience, as described by Shapin and Schaffer (1987).

Both in describing what we did in using the pump and in comparing it with the seventeenth-century experience, we find we need to define, explore and develop a number of concepts. We look again at the concept of "closure" (Collins 1981), and its relationship to "black boxing" and "delegation" (Latour 1987). We show the application of the concept of "microworld," which is another version of the notion of ideal bureaucracy discussed in the last chapter. We again discuss the crucial notion of "indifference"; we find we need to differentiate between "theoretical indifference," which coexists with polimorphic actions, and "behavioral indifference," which underlies mimeomorphic actions. We also develop the concepts of "active closure" and "passive closure" and of "mechanization." We conclude that understanding the historical development of a device such as the air pump requires us to separate the process of closure of debate from the process of mechanization, and separate them from both black boxing and delegation. Mechanization is not the direct consequence of closure even though it often follows chronologically; consensual science prior to mechanization is in a state of active closure; post mechanization we find passive closure. In the course of the chapter we make use of these concepts to sketch out a story about air pumps. We do not claim this to be history proper; rather, it is a model of what a history of a mechanical device might be like if it were informed by the theoretical structure we are trying to develop.

We used two methods to find out what it was like to operate a modern vacuum pump. We looked at pumps and operated one ourselves, tape-recording and making extensive notes of our successes and failures in following the instructions printed on the front of one of the devices. We also obtained the services of a "proxy stranger" to follow the same instructions while we looked on. This helped us understand what we were doing.[1]

1. Proxy strangers are less culturally familiar with the environment under investigation than are the researchers themselves. Thus researchers are able to notice some things that they had "taken for granted" about their knowledge through the proxy stranger's mistakes and questions; researchers might be too familiar with the cultural environment to notice these things, even with the most assiduous phenomenological introspection. The idea is that researchers will have enough knowledge to know which of the proxy stranger's mistakes are of interest, whereas to the complete stranger the world encountered is too confusing to make any kind of sense.

While the "we" in this chapter refers to Collins and Kusch, it was Collins alone who observed the proxy stranger. The methodology of the proxy stranger is set out in greater detail in Collins (1992).

Understanding peoples' relationship to a mechanical device requires one to know a little of their cultural capabilities: the first-named author is a sociologist who has spent various periods in physics laboratories, so the language of physics is not unfamiliar to him; he had, however, not operated a vacuum pump since he was at high school more than thirty years before. The second author is a philosopher with no previous experience of the modern physics laboratory. Our proxy stranger, a lecturer in social work, was a self-confessed scientific ignoramus who had done no science since he was sixteen years old.

Modern Air Pumps

Nowadays there is nothing sacred about air pumps. One Wednesday, after lunch, without making an appointment, we (the authors) strolled into the physics department at the University of Bath and asked a technician, Bob Draper, if he could show us how to use a vacuum pump. In a matter-of-fact way Draper led us to a laboratory and dragged a pump out from an untidy jumble of machinery on the floor (figure 9.1). Draper pointed out the features of the device. It could be said to consist of three units. The first was a rotary pump; to speak loosely, this is the direct descendant of Boyle's device. Today's rotary pump is cuboid, about 15 cm in each dimension, and attached to a cylinder of similar dimensions—the motor that drives it. The second unit was a "diffusion pump." This is similar in size but looks more like the cylinder head of a motorcycle,

Figure 9.1
Two vacuum pumps in a physics laboratory.

with many cooling fins. On top of this was the third unit—a vertical stainless steel cylinder about 30 cm tall and 10 cm in diameter. This was a cold trap. It was, so Draper explained, an annular device, the sleeve of which could be filled with liquid nitrogen so as to freeze vapors and permanently remove them from the residual gas.

Draper explained to us how he would operate the device, showing the sequence of valve openings and closings that would connect first the rotary pump to the vessel to be evacuated, and then the diffusion pump. The rotary pump would extract the bulk of the air—down to about .1 torr (mm of mercury)—and the diffusion pump, aided by the cold trap, would finish the job. Most of Draper's description was concerned with the sequencing and timing of switching and valve opening—something we found difficult to remember. The main problem of operating the pump, he explained, was knowing how to cure leaks and spot other anomalies. For example, a hair caught between the rubber seal and the seating of the vacuum chamber would be sufficient to cause a leakage; if the oil in the diffusion pump was old, it would take a long time to heat up to the point where it could be used efficiently.

Draper then showed us other vacuum pumps. There were six within a few yards of each other. The second one we looked at had gauges that showed the pressure inside the vessel. With this one, he explained, one did not need to control the timing of the valve-opening sequence—rather one referred to the pressure gauge; the rotary pump should be left on until the gauge registered .1 torr, and then one should switch to the diffusion pump. The third pump bore not only gauges but also a set of instructions explaining the proper sequence of valve openings and closings. All these pumps were a couple of decades old.

The fourth pump was a very new and much more highly automated device. It was designed to be "foolproof." We asked one of the regular users if it ever failed. He said it never had, though on one occasion it *appeared* to have failed. What had happened was that the vacuum gauge had been reading incorrectly. The "Penning" gauge measured extent of vacuum by reference to the electrical conductivity between two electrodes. The electrodes were separated by an insulator, and it could happen that the insulator would become coated with the breakdown products of gases being evacuated from the chamber. In this case the gauge would register anomalously high conductivity and therefore an anomalously low vacuum. This had happened recently, but it had been corrected by cleaning the gauge.

The fifth and sixth pumps were small versions of different designs.

What Is It Like to Use a Modern Vacuum Pump?

Our attention was captured by the third pump with its sequence of instructions. Draper agreed that we could be "let loose" on it. We asked Draper to watch over us as we tried to follow the instructions on air pump number three. He agreed to say nothing unless we asked, or unless he saw us about to do something that would cause damage or danger.

Air pump number three stood on a trolley at roughly desktop height. The principle components (there was no cold trap) were housed in a sheet-metal cuboid box with sides about 50 cm long. Below the box, supported by a lower platform, was a metallic green device that looked like what we had learned to see as a rotary pump and its motor. This was connected to the box by branching copper tubes (figure 9.2). The box was covered in switches and valves, and revealed two dials. A metal plate screwed to the front bore instructions (figure 9.3).

Except for the two commands about turning the cooling water on and off, these instructions were printed in silver on the black metal plate. The cooling water instructions had been added more recently in the form of strips of red "Dymotape." Without the Dymotape strips it is unlikely that we would have obeyed "NOTE 2," at the bottom of the list, which comprised the only other advice about cooling water.

In addition there were numerous "homemade" Dymotape or "Letraset" labels associated with the various valves and switches distributed over the front and left side of the box. We set out to "follow the instructions."

Turn on Cooling Water

We began the process of turning on the cooling water by noting that a clear plastic pipe emerged from the back of the pump and was attached to a tap close by. Another clear plastic pipe, putatively the return pipe, exited from the back of the device and ended at the sink. We turned on the tap and noted that water flowed out of the return pipe. Discovering

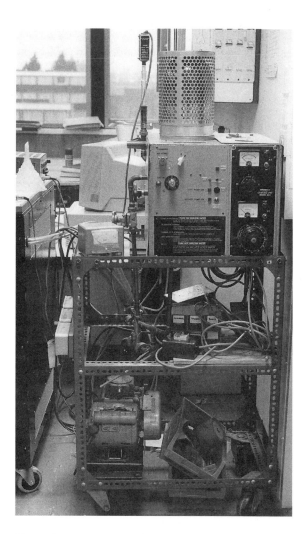

Figure 9.2
Vacuum pumps with instructions.

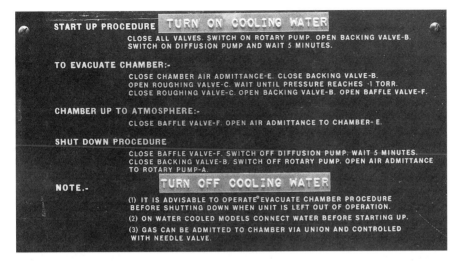

START UP PROCEDURE TURN ON COOLING WATER
CLOSE ALL VALVES. SWITCH ON ROTARY PUMP. OPEN BACKING VALVE-B.
SWITCH ON DIFFUSION PUMP AND WAIT 5 MINUTES.

TO EVACUATE CHAMBER:-
CLOSE CHAMBER AIR ADMITTANCE-E. CLOSE BACKING VALVE-B.
OPEN ROUGHING VALVE-C. WAIT UNTIL PRESSURE REACHES ·1 TORR.
CLOSE ROUGHING VALVE-C. OPEN BACKING VALVE-B. OPEN BAFFLE VALVE-F.

CHAMBER UP TO ATMOSPHERE:-
CLOSE BAFFLE VALVE-F. OPEN AIR ADMITTANCE TO CHAMBER- E.

SHUT DOWN PROCEDURE
CLOSE BAFFLE VALVE-F. SWITCH OFF DIFFUSION PUMP. WAIT 5 MINUTES.
CLOSE BACKING VALVE-B. SWITCH OFF ROTARY PUMP. OPEN AIR ADMITTANCE
TO ROTARY PUMP-A.

NOTE.- TURN OFF COOLING WATER
(1) IT IS ADVISABLE TO OPERATE EVACUATE CHAMBER PROCEDURE
BEFORE SHUTTING DOWN WHEN UNIT IS LEFT OUT OF OPERATION.
(2) ON WATER COOLED MODELS CONNECT WATER BEFORE STARTING UP.
(3) GAS CAN BE ADMITTED TO CHAMBER VIA UNION AND CONTROLLED
WITH NEEDLE VALVE.

Figure 9.3
The instructions.

the method of turning on the cooling water rested on experience and a degree of native wit. We had to "work out" what to do, and then to satisfy ourselves that we had done it correctly by listening to the gurgling noise of the water and noting the flow of water out of the "return pipe."[2] Finding and turning on the tap was not very hard, as we knew all about taps from experience, not only of laboratories, but also of domestic sinks and baths.

We discovered through observing our proxy stranger (who tried to run the pump a couple of days later), that we either knew, or had learned from Draper's brief introduction, far more about what these instructions meant than we had realized. The stranger at first saw "CLOSE ALL VALVES. SWITCH ON ROTARY PUMP. OPEN BACKING VALVE B" as an elaboration of the instruction "TURN ON COOLING WATER." He thought these were instructions telling him *how* to turn on the cooling water. Either Draper's initial explanation, or our existing know-how, had

2. Amerine and Bilmes (1979, p. 5), suggest that "Successfully following instructions can be described as constructing a course of action such that, having done this course of action, the instruction will serve as a descriptive account of what has been done" (quoted in Suchman 1987, p. 102).

made it clear *to us* that the rotary pump was something that produced a vacuum, not something that pumped water, and that is why we did not make that mistake.

Far more of the physics and mechanics of the apparatus than we realized has to be known before even the purpose and sequence of the instructions could be understood. The conventions of spacing and grouping of instructions is less unambiguous than we had noticed when we were operating the pump ourselves.

Close All Valves

Before we could close all valves we had to find "all valves" and discover what "closing a valve" consisted of. We had two ways of discovering valves; one way was by reading the rough labels stuck alongside various projections sticking out of the sheet-metal box; the other way had to do with our knowledge of what one might call "the language of valves." A valve is supposed to look like something we are intended to turn. If it is physically designed to be easy for the hand to turn, then so much the better (Norman 1988). One familiar design of valve has a stalk with a mushroomlike wheel at the end. On the side of the box there were two of these: one had a black plastic wheel with a milled edge to increase grip (a design often found on old-fashioned radiators); the other had a silver metal wheel with obvious indentations to increase the purchase of the fingers while turning (figure 9.4). These were labeled respectively "Backing Valve B" and "Roughing Valve C."[3]

Collins gripped the Roughing Valve valve-wheel and rotated it clockwise (the conventional closing direction), though a few degrees against firm pressure. It was not clear whether or not this comprised "closing" the valve. To determine whether this was indeed "closing" the valve, Collins decided to experiment with "opening." Reversing the direction he discovered that after a few degrees of stiff movement, the wheel would rotate easily though more than a full turn before encountering stiffness again. He concluded that this was "opening" and therefore the reverse

3. We say "labeled," but what we mean is that there were such labels on the surface of the sheet-metal box and they seemed to apply to these valves according to the conventional spatial arrangements between objects and their labels.

Figure 9.4
Side of the pump with valves and labels.

movement was "closing." The few degrees of movement against firm pressure that he had first taken to be "closing" must have been (unnecessary) "tightening," the confusion being brought about by trying to follow an instruction to close an already closed valve. We now understood the envelope of movements within which valve operation must take place. Depending on this, Collins discovered that Backing Valve B was also already closed.

This experience was now used to resolve a dilemma concerning Baffle Valve F. The label bearing the appropriate legend appeared to be next to an object which, if it was a valve, broke all the semiotic rules of valveness. There was no stalk, no wheel, and nothing for the hand to grip. On the face of it, Baffle Valve F was a piece of smooth stainless tubing about 2 cm in diameter emerging at about 15 degrees off a right angle, through the sheet-metal wall of the box (figure 9.5).

This tube spoke the language of liquid or gas transport and invited a further tube to be connected to its end. The assembler of the device had understood the problem, because, close to the alphabetical label, a curving, double-ended "Letraset," arrow suggested rotation; there was no such label on the other valves. Collins grasped the tube and found that it would rotate about its long axis with roughly the same degree of movement as the other two valves—a full turn or so in either direction with a small possibility of "tightening" at both limits. This convinced us that the tube was indeed a "language-deficient" valve. Rotating it fully clockwise, we concluded we had "closed all valves." (This was a mistake, as it turned out, since we had had not noticed that there was a valve "A" somewhere else entirely. Fortunately, it too was already closed.)

Switch on Rotary Pump. Open Backing Valve B. Switch on Diffusion Pump and Wait Five Minutes

We found an electrical switch labeled "rotary pump" associated with a red "telltale" light. We switched it in the conventional direction for "on" in Britain—from up to down.[4] The telltale did not light. We concluded that the main power source was not switched on. Collins tried a number of switches on the front panel of the box, but to no effect. At this point

---

4. In the United States the convention is opposite.

Figure 9.5
Baffle valve F.

Draper suggested we trace the electrical wire coming out of the box; we discovered it led to a loose plug. All the wall sockets were occupied, but Draper removed a plug, freeing a socket for us. Like a cook knowing his or her way around a kitchen, Draper knew his way around the lab; Draper had "local knowledge" whereas we did not. We would not have known which plug it was permissible to pull from a socket. After plugging in, we tried the rotary pump switch again, and this time the light came on and the pump burst into life with a satisfactory whirring and plopping sound. On opening Backing Valve B, the sound changed to a deeper note, suggesting that the pump was doing more sucking work. Now we threw the switch marked "Diffusion Pump" and noted that its associated telltale light came on. We noted the time and relaxed for five minutes.

The End of the Story

So far we have described only a small part of the process of making a vacuum in terms of logical sequence, degree of difficulty, and time spent on the observations. But for the purposes of this chapter it is enough. More detailed description of the trials and tribulations involved in completing the task would needlessly reiterate examples of problems and actions of which we already have a sufficient store. Suffice it to say that after working and worrying for another half-hour or so, and with a degree of help from Bob Draper, we succeeded in making a vacuum. We will now reanalyze, in a more formal way, what we had done up to this point.

The Actions So Far

Turn on Cooling Water

The nature of what we had so far accomplished can be described under the heading of our two main types of actions. Turning on the cooling water was accomplished largely with easy (for us) polimorphic actions drawing on commonsense knowledge. It required us to recognize the sort of pipes that carry water, to understand about taps and flows of water, to know the sound that running water makes, to follow the direction of the pipes from the back of the box to the sink, and to turn on the tap. The action as a whole is the sort of thing that one would expect to carry out in many different ways on different occasions depending upon how things had been arranged in the laboratory—how matters were disposed as a result of interaction with the social and technological environment. For example, we might have had to locate the end of the water pipes and attach one to the tap and lower the other into the sink; we might have had to move the whole apparatus close to the sink; we might have discovered that the pump used a reservoir of water with a gravity feed, and that the first thing to be done was to fill the feeder tank; we might have discovered that the pump had a recirculating system with a radiator (like a car engine), and that there was a water pump to be turned on as part of turning on the cooling water. It might even be that to turn on the cooling water, one must first employ the services of a person to lift water from an irrigation ditch with a shadoof. The list of things that we might have had to do in order to turn on the cooling water is open-ended, and the distinction between these different things would have been important to us if the cooling water was to be successfully turned on in each different circumstance. In this case, we had to discover the circumstances in which we actually found ourselves, and to respond accordingly.

Turning on the tap was different. We did not care if we turned the tap fast or slow, or with our left hands or our right hands. We were "behaviorally indifferent" to tap turning even though we were not behaviorally indifferent to "turning on the cooling water." Turning on the cooling water was a polimorphic action, while turning on the tap was a mimeomorphic action. The standard action of tap turning is ubiquitous across cultures, and repetitive.

Behavioral indifference is not the same as lack of attention or unconsciousness to our actions. On the one hand, with a special effort of attention, we can describe in detail things, such as turning on the tap, to which we are behaviorally indifferent; on the other hand, we often pay no attention to things about which we are not behaviorally indifferent (the standard example is driving our cars on our regular journey to work). To discover whether there is behavioral indifference to what we do we can ask whether we would be happy to have it carried out in exactly the same way every time.

Behavioral indifference to an action is not fixed for all time. Thus, though we were not behaviorally indifferent to "turning on the cooling water," we would have become behaviorally indifferent to it if we had to use the same pump, in the same laboratory, over and over again. On each occasion of "turning on the cooling water *on Pump 3*" we would have been happy to see it carried out in "exactly" the same way. What is more, on subsequent occasions, turning on the cooling water on Pump 3 would cease to require us to engage creatively with the organization of the laboratory because we could just repeat what we had done before (within our envelope of indifference). Thus, "turning on cooling water for a pump" remains a polimorphic action whereas "turning on cooling water for Pump 3" becomes a mimeomorphic action. Of course, if things changed between visits, or something broke, turning on the cooling water for this pump would once more require polimorphic actions. We might try to do it as a mimeomorphic action, but it would be unlikely to be a success executed that way.

Close All Valves

Closing all the valves required us first to discover the movements required to close a valve, and to discover what counted as a valve. What we had to do was transform the side of the box as we found it into something that had three discrete objects sticking out of it called "valves." Two of these valves were designed in such a way as to make it easy for us to pick them out, given that we shared in some ubiquitous cultural competences in the recognition of everyday objects. The third valve required quite a lot more work. One might say of the third, that we had to repair its symbolic defects. Or we might say that we had to allow an unusual area of tolerance around the appearance of valveness in order to allow ourselves to see that little bit of the world as a valve.

Once we had the valves classified, and once we had learned the outside envelope of the range of movements that could comprise a valve closing, little was involved in the actual closing. It is quite irrelevant, once more, to discuss the speed at which we turned the wheels, the *exact* torque we exerted on them, the time it took to close each one, the elapsed time between closing one and closing another, the hand we used to turn the valve, the position of our feet and our heads while turning, and so forth. We were indifferent to all of this. We were indifferent to it in the sense that we would have been perfectly happy had the valves been turned in a variety of ways (in terms of the above parameters), or in the identical way each time (to as fine a degree as we were able to detect). What this means is that "valve closing" was just like "turning on the cooling water." For us, on this occasion, it was a polimorphic action, involving interaction with the social world of valve design, terminating at the foot of the action path with a mimeomorphic action. "Closing all valves" was a polimorphic action, whereas closing each individual valve was mimeo-morphic.

Once more, with repeated work on the same pump, even the element of polimorphic action involved with our first valve closings could have been successfully executed mimeomorphically.

Switch on Rotary Pump

Switching on the rotary pump required first a bit of polimorphic action of the same sort as was required to turn on the cooling water—that is, find the plug, and turn on the main power—then a bit of classification of the front panel of the box—that is, find the switch that switched on the pump, which involved interaction with the cultural world of the design of mechanisms. But, that done, toggling the rotary pump switch is characterized by our indifference to the particular way it was behaviorally instantiated—it is mimeomorphic.

Boyle's Experience

Since the rotary pump is the successor to Boyle's device, it is worth dwelling on the contrast between what he needed to do and what we did. In the 1660s Boyle's use of an air pump required one or two strong men to operate the cylinder and work the valves on each stroke (according to Shapin and Schaffer, self-acting valves did not appear for another fifteen years). Shapin and Schaffer describe the operation of Boyle's pump as follows:

At the upper lip of the cylinder there was a small hole into which a brass valve could be inserted as required. Within the cylinder was a wooden piston (or "sucker"), topped with "a good thick piece of tanned show-leather" which provided for an exceedingly tight fit between piston and the inside of the cylinder. The piston was worked up and down by means of an iron rack and pinion device. . . .

. . . with the stopcock in the closed position and the valve inserted the sucker was drawn up to the top of the cylinder; at this point there was no air between sucker and the top of cylinder. Then the sucker was drawn down and the stopcock was opened, permitting the passage of a quantity of air from the receiver into the cylinder. The stopcock was closed, the valve was removed, and the sucker was forced up, thus expelling that quantity of air to the exterior. The process was repeated, each "exsuction" requiring progressively more force. (Shapin and Schaffer, 1987, p. 28)

The question of the goodness of fit between piston and cylinder was a matter of continual attention:

. . . he [Boyle] took special pains to recount how the leather ring around the sucker was lubricated, both to facilitate its movement in the cylinder and to "more exactly hinder the air from insinuating itself betwixt it and the sides of the cylinder": a certain quantity of "sallad oil" was poured into both receiver [i.e., vacuum chamber] and into the cylinder, and more oil was used to lubricate and seal the valve. Boyle noted that sometimes a mixture of oil and water proved a more effective seal and lubricant. (p. 29)

The special attention to the seal was doubly important because Boyle's main critic, Hobbes, argued that the impossibility of sealing this space took the force from Boyle's conclusions. Hobbes said that though the seal might keep out "straw and feathers" it was impossible for it to keep out air because the force of pumping must distort the brass cylinder, because the slightest "hard atom" insinuating itself between leather and cylinder would make sufficient space to allow air to pass, and because experience suggested that leather was never enough to act as a perfect seal against air or water.[5]

Shapin and Schaffer (p. 43) describe one of Boyle's first experiments to note the effect of his pump on the height of mercury in an inverted tube (the effect on the Torricellian space). The height of the mercury column diminished on the first suck, and continued to diminish on each successive suck until, after a quarter of an hour of pumping, it would diminish no further. We may be sure that during this operation there was painstaking attention paid to the seals, the "sallad oil," the speed at which the workers moved the cylinder handles, and so forth. We may be sure that had we been able to disturb Boyle (or, at least, his assistants), at any moment during the course of this "action path," he would have been able to report on the progress of all these features of the process of evacuation. These features for Boyle and for Hobbes were not matters of behavioral indifference.

In 1992 what did we do to effect all this and more? We followed the instruction "switch on rotary pump." The question of the nature of the seals and the speed of the pumping were all so much a matter of complete

---

5. Something that Boyle could not answer by any technological means, because Hobbes took air to be infinitely fluid.

indifference to us that we cannot say anything about it. We had no more concern with how these things happened than we had with the speed of movement of the toggle of the electrical switch that switched the pump on. From the seventeenth century to now, these activities had become, first, with the closure of the debate about the meaning of the air pump experiments, matters of *theoretical indifference* but, nevertheless, matters involving polimorphic actions still demanding the attention of those who actually worked the pump and, only much later, matters of behavioral indifference, ready to be mechanized.

A Reconstructed "History" of the Air Pump in Terms of Actions

Over the course of a half-hour or so, we novices were able to follow instructions and make what is nowadays called a vacuum. We have seen that it was not easy, and that it rested on various skills that normally go unnoticed. For example, understanding an instruction is skill-laden, as became clear through watching our proxy stranger.[6] What makes this less obvious than it might otherwise be is the ubiquity of linguistic and related socialization. Ubiquitous skills become invisible.[7]

6. For earlier analyses of the use of instructions and their embeddedness in the background of social competences, see Collins (1990), chap. 8, and Suchman (1987). Suchman says:

. . . there is no reason to believe that if a person has a set of instructions for operating a machine, and we generate a description of the activity of operating a machine from watching a person, that the description we generate should look anything like the instructions. In fact, if our description of the situated activity does mirror the structure of the instructions, there is reason to believe that something is amiss. (p. 111)

A set of instructions is a kind of machine. It is a machine that attempts to replace a human "coach," someone who is there to guide one's actions, continually responding to the particular situation as it develops. The failures of a list of instructions seen as a machine are the failures of our attempts to replace ordinary interactive language with a linguistic mechanism. (For more on failures to follow instructions, see Suchman, especially chap. 7.)

We would argue that there are occasions when instructions can be followed unproblematically. This is when the human (or pigeon) has been drilled into a mimeomorphic response (see below).

7. We have explained this in our treatment of McDonald's and in our use of the idea of "RAT." For a further elaboration of this point, see Collins (1997). One

Even granted our various skills, we still needed some help from Draper.[8] Nevertheless, it was easier for us than it would have been for Boyle and his assistants. How is it that relatively ignorant visitors to a physics laboratory are able to follow instructions as successfully as this? And can we find an explanation that will show how it is that we still needed some help?

Closure, Black Boxing, Delegation, and All That

Some would say that the difference between Boyle's air pump and the modern vacuum pumps that we have been describing is a matter of "black boxing" or "delegation" of responsibility to machinery.[9] This will not do. It would not be an incorrect redescription of what had happened, it would even be a soothing way of putting things (because it would make us feel as though we understood something of the process), but it is only a redescription in summary terms; it explains little or nothing and it captures none of the complexities of actions described above nor the residual problems.

Again, it is useful to start with an analysis of terms. "Black boxing" and "closure" are often used synonymously. One may trace the origin of this way of thinking at least as far back as Collins (1975). There it was argued that agreement about the detection of gravitational radiation was coextensive with the agreement about what constituted a good gravity

---

might say that "intelligent machines" are our collective proxy strangers as regards language. Their poor linguistic performance continually reminds us of the depth and inscrutability of our linguistic abilities.

8. Many of our failures, it has to be said, had to do with mistakes in the instructions in relation to this particular rebuilt pump. If the pump had still been in the form for which the instructions were designed, and if the "5 minute" instruction had read "10 minutes," we believe we would have lowered the pressure to .01 torr first time around with less assistance from Draper, though we would still have needed some help. (This is also what Draper told us.) We would, we suspect, have remained in ignorance about what it was we had lowered to .01 torr, but, on the other hand, we would not have been made so nicely aware of the digitizing work required to recognize the objects to which instructions referred; this awareness was partly a consequence of misdesign, especially of the Baffle Valve.

9. This is how it might be described by Bruno Latour (1987) and his followers.

wave detector. Thus the acceptance of the general principle of design of an instrument coincided with closure of scientific debate about the existence of the phenomenon with which the instrument was meant to interact. This process was likened to ships being put into bottles. The instrument, once "bottled" could be used relatively unproblematically in subsequent work just as, say, voltmeters were used relatively unproblematically in the gravity wave controversy. Of course, if a controversy deepened, any bottle could have its ship removed again.

This point is generalized into a whole sociological philosophy by Bruno Latour, using the term "black box" instead of the ship-in-bottle metaphor.[10] Latour links "black boxing" to power and then to automation. But, *if debates are closed through the exercise of power, as in* the kind

---

10. As Latour (1987) puts it:

. . . no distinction has been made between what is called a "scientific" fact and what is called a "technical" object or artifact. This division, although traditional and convenient, artificially cuts through the question of how to ally oneself to resist controversies. The problem of the builder of "fact" is the same as that of the builder of "objects": how to convince others, how to control their behavior, how to gather sufficient resources in one place, how to have the claim or the object spread out in time and space. In both cases, it is others who have the power to transform the claim or the object into a durable whole. . . . But . . . the only way for a whole stable field of science to be mobilized in other fields, is for it to be turned into an automaton, a machine, one more piece of equipment in a lab, another black box. Technics and sciences are so much the same phenomenon that I was right to use the same term black box, even loosely, to designate their outcome. (p. 131)

He goes on to point to a difference in the way what he calls "science" and "technology" present themselves, which stresses the essential similarity between social control and mechanization:

Yet, despite this impossibility of distinguishing between science and technics, it is still possible to detect, in the process of enrolling allies and controlling their behavior, two *moments* that will allow the reader to remain closer to common sense by retaining some difference between "science" and "technology." The first moment is when new and unexpected allies are recruited—and this is most often visible in laboratories, in scientific and technical literature, in heated discussions; the second moment is when all the gathered resources are made to act as one unbreakable whole—and this is more often visible in engines, machines and pieces of hardware. This is the only distinction that may be drawn between "sciences" and "technics" if we want to shadow scientists and engineers as they build their subtle and versatile alliances. (p. 132)

of theory espoused in the sociology of scientific knowledge,[11] then machines are made to work through the exercise of power. It cannot also be that the exercise of power is made possible simply because machines work.[12] At the very least, one needs some prior explanation of the working of machines, or an understanding of the special circumstances in which they seem to become independent of those who make them. In terms of the framework of the sociology of scientific knowledge, automation is a problem, not a solution.[13] The empirical counterpart of this theoretical argument is to be seen wherever it turns out that an instrument, whose use has been accepted and whose general principles of design have been settled, still requires skill and agreement to make it work (as in this case). This is *active closure*. To avoid the need for active closure—to get to *passive closure*—something additional is necessary; the something additional is immensely puzzling *precisely because* of the social theory of closure.[14]

Consider the air pump once more (here we begin to take serious liberties with the history). There was once, let us say, an open debate—the two sides represented by Boyle and Hobbes—about whether or not there was such a thing as a vacuum. Coextensive with this debate was a debate about the meaning and design of air pumps. The big argument about the design of air pumps was closed coextensively with what we might call the victory of the Boyle side over the Hobbes side. A well-designed air pump became an air pump that would cause the lowering of a column of mercury with a Torricellian space above it or some such. We can say that this lowering came to define a "vacuum."

11. This includes the main thrust of works such as Latour and Woolgar (1979).

12. The same point could be made about the idea of the spread of tools as a source of stability in society. See Strum and Latour (1978).

13. Collins (1975, 1985, 1990) argues that the social nature of closure makes it difficult to see how any machine can work. Latour's solution is to take the semiotic turn and grant power to machines. The problems associated with this move are argued out in contributions by Collins, Yearley, Latour, and Callon in Pickering (1992).

14. For another recent critique of Latour's approach, see Ramsey (1992). Ramsey distinguishes between "ontological black boxes" (devices), and "epistemological black boxes," which are the unproblematic use of such devices. For similar

If we take even more historical liberties we can imagine Hobbes in a laboratory with his own pump and his own team of strong and skilled helpers. We can also imagine them doing experiments on the spring of the gross constituents of the air without, as far as they were concerned, producing vacuums. We may imagine that their experimental program, and perhaps even the details of their design of pump, would be a little different from Boyle's. (Perhaps the Hobbes team would be less concerned with the fit of the sucker into the cylinder, since Hobbes believed small leaks were unavoidable.) With the closure of the debate, the Hobbesian way of doing things, along with the associated skills of Hobbes's assistants, would become redundant to the scientific community. The proper design of an air pump would become, without dispute, the Boyle design.

But notice that in this scenario Boyle's air pump still requires the services of strong and skilled men to work it; it still requires the manual removal and replacement of the valve stopper, and it still requires careful and continuous attention to the state of the leather, the diachylon, and the "sallad oil" even though there is no longer any doubt that these do produce "a vacuum" when properly handled. In short, Boyle's assistants still need the same skills after closure as they required before closure. In this scenario the "scientific community's" growing *theoretical indifference* to the way vacuums are produced does not translate into indifference to the behaviors required to produce the vacuum on the part of Boyle's assistants; the assistants are not *behaviorally indifferent* to the working of the pump.[15] The only reduction of skill involved in the closure is that Boyle and his allies no longer have to argue so well.

The imagined postclosure scenario is close to the truth in this respect: that the air pump remained a thing of wonder and artifice for many years. This is documented by Shapin and Schaffer. There were very few air pumps in existence for several decades, and there were correspondingly

---

criticisms of Latour's over-heavy reliance on the notion that inscription devices are closed, see, for example, Collins and Yearley (1992).

15. Where there had once been alternative ways of seeing the world, and it required every kind social and rhetorical skill to maintain them, now the maintenance of Boyle's view needs less work.

few people who could understand, maintain, and work them. There are more air pumps in the University of Bath today than there were in the whole world in 1670. The six we saw within a few yards of one another in a single physics laboratory are more than there were in England at the same date. As we have shown, and will show, the air pump story is not over; pumps are still not completely automated; they still require a degree of active closure, yet there is no questioning the possibility of vacuums.

Let us look at this another way: when the postclosure Boyle commands his assistants to "produce a vacuum" they will do so, perhaps using this pump, perhaps another. So far as Boyle is concerned, that is all there is to it. Consider, on the other hand, ourselves in relationship to the rotary pump that has descended from Boyle's device: we switch on a switch on this pump or that pump and the vacuum is produced. Superficially, both we and Boyle are in the same position with respect to vacuums; to produce a vacuum we each do the same thing—we set in motion a "machine." We may even be equally indifferent to the way we set the machine in motion: in Boyle's case it might be with a few curt syllables or a written instruction; in our case a fast or a slow movement of the switch. But these are two very different kinds of machines in terms of the action cascades required to produce the vacuum. In the case of Boyle, he depends on the polimorphic actions of his assistants. He depends on their skills of repair, both literal and metaphorical. Boyle's assistants have to have cultural competences as well as obedience; there has to be more than Boyle's power to compel his assistants' assent; his assistants have to have the ability to do what he wants and make the right choices in respect of the varying world of glassblowers, diachylon makers, leather tanners, and so forth. Boyle could substitute for his assistants neither ignorant slaves nor trained pigeons, however much power he had over them.

In our case, we depend on no skills and no polimorphic actions in the rotary pump; we could, in principle, train pigeons to push the rotary pump round and round. In terms of an analysis of types of actions in the cascade, theoretical indifference is a very different thing from behavioral indifference, though this may not appear so to the scientist distanced from the laboratory, nor to the analyst distanced from the practical problems of automation.

The Spread of Esoteric Skills

Given that black boxing, or delegation, cannot explain the spread of the vacuum, what can explain it? There are three elements to the process: the spread of esoteric skills, making pumps touch ubiquitous skills, behavior digitization, and mechanization. The first step in the spread of the air pump was a spreading out of the skills of design, maintenance, and operation. More people were shown the recipe for "Diachylon," more were shown how to make a leather seal, more were introduced to the esoterica of "sallad oil" and water, more were shown how and when to pump, how to avoid damage and distortion, how to seal cracks with a stinking mixture of cheese parings and lead oxide, what to watch for, how to know if the pump was leaking, how long it took to produce a satisfactory vacuum, and when to stop and search for problems. We could, as far as the theory of the nature and distribution of knowledge is concerned, have air pumps throughout our universities producing vacuums as in Boyle's day. The economics of this mode of spread is against it, but if they had spread out in this way, the air pump would be just as closed in the theoretical sense. Air pump operation would still, however, be invested with skills—skills of repair, both literal (repairing the leather seals and so forth) and metaphorical. Metaphorical repair would mean *actively* interpreting every apparent failure of the pump as a human or technical failure, not a failure of the theory and idea of the pump.

Lest this seem fanciful, note that there are other devices with these characteristics scattered throughout our universities. For example, the widespread apparatus that reproduces Millikan's measurements of the charge on the electron is notoriously difficult to use. It seems to require about the same level of skill and active repair as Millikan applied when he first used his own apparatus. There is, then, no firm link between our ability to capture skills in mechanisms and our ability to enforce interpretations of the world.

What is more, some of this type of active closure is still going on even in the case of vacuum pumps. When we failed, first time, to get down to .01 torr we did not start to wonder whether there really are vacuums, we repaired the vacuum chamber, literally,[16] and repaired the failure

16. A later part of the story, which we have not gone into in this chapter.

metaphorically. When, as was reported to us, the automatic "pump 4" appeared to fail, it was the Penning gauge that was literally repaired and the notion of vacuum that has descended from Boyle's work that was metaphorically repaired. These are cases where the substitution of skills by mechanisms was not working to full effect.[17]

Note again that to the extent to which pumps need their users to be skilled, they are not doing any *compelling*. There was nothing compelling about the dozen or so air pumps that were to be found in the world in the decade after the closure of the debate with Hobbes. On the contrary, one had to work hard at knowing how to use them if they were to produce a vacuum. All the compulsion had to come out of what would become the socially enforced certainty that Boyle's pump produced a vacuum. And one can see the extent to which this is still true, even in our use of a modern air pump. If we had not believed it ought to produce a vacuum, we would not have succeeded. The difficult and complicated thing is to explain how the mechanisms helped at all.[18]

Making Pumps That Touch Ubiquitous Skills

The second step in the history of the growing ubiquity of air pumps was the substitution of esoteric skills by mechanisms of a sort that made it possible for the machine to make contact with the cultural world of users whose training was less specific and who, therefore, seemed less well trained. The ability to read the instructions, skilled activity though we have shown it to be, is almost ubiquitous in the English-speaking world;

---

17. That even modern pumps need skill to operate would have been still more clear had we chosen a harder pump to work with. Collins had, as it happens, already had some contact with one of the other six pumps we were shown—a glass diffusion pump made in Bath's glassblowing workshops. This was how he described his use of that pump some three or four years earlier:

The diffusion pump is a complex array of glassware with oil bubbling and dripping through it. It behaved in terrifying ways; I never did work out what was going on. I would not be able to use a diffusion pump without considerable extra instruction. (Collins 1990, p. 163) [Collins should have said "this diffusion pump" rather than "a diffusion pump."]

18. The primary scientific experience of those who believe in the unproblematic nature of inscription devices, apparatus, and microworlds is often in biology. In biochemistry laboratories there just *are* more of the kind of machines that mimic

it is, once more, like the skills of McDonald's counter clerks and their customers. Valve closing and opening is ubiquitous wherever there are taps and central heating. Just as with a satisfactory expert system, a satisfactory set of instructions on a machine must make contact with the cultural world of the user, and it is more likely to be successful if it is directed toward areas of ubiquitous culture (common sense), and away from areas of narrowly distributed expertise. Making machines that make contact with more widely distributed expertise is another part of what has been misleadingly lumped into notions such as black boxing or delegation. (This is not to say that the range of ubiquitous skills is not continually being updated, and that the designers of new technologies do not contribute to the "ubiquitization" or new skills, nor that a quotient of esoteric skills are usually required to operate even the most "automatic" of machines.)

Mechanization

The third part of the process *is* automation, or mechanization proper. This begins with changing the nature of some of the skills needed to operate bits of the pump so that *behaviors,* not skills, can be mimicked by the machine. There are no skills embedded in the automated air pumps of today, only mechanisms that mimic behaviors. The pumps can mimic just those human skills that can be substituted by behaviors; these are not the skills once used by Boyle's technicians. What has happened is that here and there Boyle's assistants' skills have been substituted by other skills of the special kind and it is some of these that have been taken over by mechanisms. The necessary initial transformation is from polimorphic to mimeomorphic actions. While closure of the debate about reciprocating air pumps happened three hundred years ago, the process

---

mimeomorphic actions—machines that shake, inject, and measure in a repetitious way. The role of the technician is often straightforward in these cases—keeping things orderly—so that the whole laboratory can take on the appearance of a mechanized world.

In the physical sciences, new experiments generally involve new and complex devices, and the division between scientist and technician is not clear cut. A new apparatus is generally designed and tended by the scientist, technicians helping with the building and the development of subunits within the overall design.

of substituting human skills with mechanical behaviors in the case of air pumps is still going on.

In our narrative we have described those parts of a modern pump that can be operated with mimeomorphic actions. We have mentioned a number of ways in which we had neither control nor interest in the operations of parts of the pump that would have been salient in the actions of Boyle and his assistants. Not everything can be delegated to the machine; the things that can be delegated are those things to which we are behaviorally indifferent. For example, we could never automate "turn on cooling water," but we could automate "turn on cooling water on Pump 3."

Incidentally, it is quite easy to imagine the rival school of Boyle and Hobbes surviving to this day, each using their own automated devices; thus we can even imagine the mechanization of pumps of rival schools without closure of the debate about vacuums, *though there would be closure within each school.* That is to say, we can imagine intraschool behavioral indifference without interschool theoretical indifference.[19]

We now want to discuss the growth of areas of indifference about the details of the operation of air pumps and the subsequent mechanization of these areas of indifference—a related but not coextensive process. We will have to invent the early stages of the story.

A "Just So" History of Air Pump Technology

Let us imagine that ten years after the closure of the debate between Boyle and Hobbes, there were enough air pumps around to allow an argument to rage between those who believed the best seals were to be achieved with "sallad oil" alone and those who believed a mixture of oil and water to be better. Settling this debate was unimportant to the future of the idea of the vacuum, since all agreed that all pumps that worked made the mercury fall and both designs produced the effect on at least some occasions. "Vacuum scientists" would be theoretically indifferent to the mixture used to seal their leather, but within this theoretical indifference we can see how we could develop a whole history and

19. There are modern disagreements where each side of the debate utilizes its own machinery. Consider for example, the "machinery" used by astrologers.

sociology of technological knowledge which took leather-sealing methods as its topic.

Suppose that debate was won by the oil-and-water mixers. Henceforth everything to be designated a satisfactory seal would have to be lubricated with a mixture and every seal found to be satisfactory would be taken to have been thus lubricated. It might still need a lot of skill to lubricate a sucker—to choose the right kind of oil, to choose the right mixture, to soak the leather for the right length of time—but it would be the case that no failures would be blamed on the fact that it was a *mixture* of oil and water that was used; where trouble threatened, the fact that a mixture was best would be repaired. There is, however, a layer of "technologists" further down where the exact proportions—50/50 or 80/20—become the subject of attention and give rise to a new controversy between skilled lubricant mixers. This might give way to a new closure around, say, 80/20. After this, the type of oil, or the length of soak prior to use, might become the subject of debate among competing virtuosi. Each of these debates could be the topic of a history or sociology of technology. At each stage we discover the potential for new arguments. The structure of the action cascade is once more like a "fractal"—at each increased level of magnification we see a scale model of the whole, or at least a potential scale model.

But, again, something interesting happens as we decrease the scale. At certain points, though there are always different ways of doing things, people cease to care. At that point the thing—it might be kid leather soaked for an hour in an 80/20 emulsion of virgin Spanish olive oil and London tap water—commands no further attention; potential debate is not opened. All variations below that level of attention are a matter of indifference to all parties, just as the variations in the way we "turned on a tap" were a matter of indifference to us. At that point the action tree become mimeomorphic and at that point the seals can be mechanized. Note again that mechanization does not happen when ways of producing a vacuum become a matter of indifference to *Boyle,* they happen where *no one* in the action cascade cares about how they execute their actions.[20]

20. Of course, as explained above, people begin to care again when things break down. But repairing broken-down things involves polimorphic actions.

Automating Modern Vacuum Pumps

Now let us return to real, contemporary vacuum pumps. Compare pump number 3 (the one we used), with pump number 4 (the automated device). To pump 4 has been delegated the mimeomorphic actions pertaining to pump 3, but *only* the mimeomorphic actions. Pump 4 cannot read instructions, and cannot classify the world of spatchcocked valves. Something has had to happen to these instructions and valves before the human skills can be substituted. We have had to arrange the taps, valves, and switches so that they can be recognized by a machine.[21] It is hard to imagine any robot with the ability to *recognize* "Baffle Valve F" as it was presented to us. But the *potential* for mechanization is there in our theoretical indifference to shape of valve wheels or handles, in spite of the skill required to recognize them. The shape of valve wheels is not part of any argument about the ability of these devices to make vacuums. What is more, the valve openings and closings and sequencings are already in a state that makes them ready to be mechanized. The existence of pump 4, then, comes as no surprise to us, but it is also not a surprise that a pump of the design of pump 4 is a recent innovation. Mechanization, compared to closure, can be, and in this case has been, a much longer process.

Everything that Boyle's assistants did, as far as he was concerned, was a candidate for mechanization, because none of it had to do with the use of vacuums in research. Over the years we have seen it happening. What we, the authors, did with pump 3 is just as much ready for mechanization. The mimeomorphic parts could be mechanized tomorrow; one may easily imagine a robot for turning each valve or for switching each switch, if not for recognizing them in the first place. With some further modifications, however, the whole process could be mechanized. What cannot yet be mechanized—even potentially—are those things for which the pump is used in a research laboratory.

Summary

The first stage of closure in any scientific debate is likely to be active closure. That is, our machines, detectors, and other apparatuses, are kept

---

21. Or design the machine to match these, and just these, valves.

closed by the constant skilled activity of "repair." An apparatus that is maintained by "active closure" requires constant skilled attention and ingenuity to maintain its place in the world. Mechanization is a separate process that is difficult to explain in the light of social theories of science. The theory of mechanization developed here is still a social theory, in that it shows that what can and cannot be mechanized is a matter of the way humans attend to the world. One can mechanize that to which one has become indifferent in a certain way.

A common mistake is to think that closure of debate gives rise to a mechanized world. To someone like our imagined Boyle, this might appear to be the case. That is, once he has beaten the imagined Hobbes, he can treat his laboratory and its associated "technicians" as a black box (or ship-in-bottle), the inside of which need no longer concern him. He merely orders up a vacuum whenever he wants one. But this black box is an action cascade stuffed full of human skills—it is very far from being an automaton. This difference is utterly clear to those who try to mechanize black boxes prematurely. A mechanized world is crucially different from, say, an ordinary bureaucracy—which is rigidly ordered but ordered via everyone's *understanding* of their place in a social hierarchy. A mechanized world is devoid of the need for social understanding, polimorphic actions, and socially situated choices. Where a mechanized world contains human beings, they have made themselves like cogs in the mechanism. We have tried to show how these ideas work out in the history of the mechanization of devices.

10

Conclusion: Dichotomies and History

Dichotomies

The distinction between polimorphic and mimeomorphic actions is different from other dichotomies. The action-morphicity dichotomy is not the same as the *action versus behavior* dichotomy central to the philosophical debate on the nature of action.[1] For the philosophers of action, the crucial division is between behaviors that are associated with an intention, and those that are not (that is, the same distinction we make between action and "mere behavior"). For us, the crucial distinction lies within the realm of intentional action and depends upon the extent to which an action can be mimicked by reproducing the behavior associated with it.

The distinction between polimorphic actions and mimeomorphic actions does not map onto the distinction between *action versus basic action*.[2] Within philosophical discourse, basic actions are the actions, at the bottom of what we call the "action tree," that we carry out in order to carry out any other action further up. But basic actions are not mimeomorphic actions because mimeomorphic actions can be found at any level of action trees. They are more populous at the bottom of action trees, but this is not part of their definition.

The *pre-predicative versus predicative, ready-to-hand versus present-to-hand,* and *being-in-the-world versus thinking-about-the-world* distinctions do not coincide with the shape of actions distinction because in

1. See for example, Dretske (1991) and chapter 3, above.
2. For example, Danto (1973).

both polimorphic and mimeomorphic actions, actors do and do not focus their conscious attention on the results and consequences of their actions.[3]

Some recent writers base their ideas on the phenomenological distinctions mentioned in the last paragraph. Unsurprisingly, the action-morphicity analysis divides actions in a different place from where these other writers divide actions. Hubert Dreyfus (1972) divides the world into *formal versus informal knowledge domains, with* only the formal being "completely formalized and calculable"; he erects a "knowledge barrier" between these domains, which prevents computers from crossing beyond the boundaries of the formal domain. But both of Dreyfus's types of knowledge domain contain both polimorphic and mimeomorphic actions, and so the realm of application of computers cuts across his domains.[4]

As can be seen from the argument of chapter 5, our division of actions is also different from that of Hubert Dreyfus and Stuart Dreyfus (1986) because their distinction depends heavily on what is *self-conscious versus intuitive;* we show that both mimeomorphic and polimorphic actions can be executed both self-consciously and in a more internalized fashion. It is clear, furthermore, that we disagree with the Dreyfusian hierarchy of skills, which runs from those driven by expressible rules to those driven by intuitive competences. While there are skills of both these types, they do not always form a hierarchy; some self-consciously executed mimeomorphic actions are very skillful and highly valued. Again, skilled actions are not always learned in the Dreyfusian sequence, from the expressible to the inexpressible.

Chapter 5 also shows that our dichotomy does not mirror Lucy Suchman's distinction between *plans versus situated actions.*[5] Thus polimorphic actions are situated actions, but canoeing down rapids, which is a situated action for Suchman, is a species of mimeomorphic action. Some of Suchman's situated actions are situated because of their physical complexity, others because of their social embedding.

3. For the a detailed account of these phenomenological distinctions, see Kusch (1989).

4. See Collins (1996).

5. Suchman (1987).

The distinction between *tacit versus propositional knowledge* also divides the world at a different place than does the action-morphicity distinction. For example, in chapter 5 we argued that bicycle riding, the classic example of tacit knowledge, has both mimeomorphic (bike balancing) and polimorphic components.[6]

Herbert Simon's distinction between the realm of *ill-structured versus well-structured problems* does not fit with polimorphic and mimeomorphic divisions because much of what we have traditionally thought of as well structured problems are well-structured only because they rest on a foundation of polimorphic "repair" work.[7]

Max Weber distinguished *actions versus social actions,* where social actions are directed at other actors. All polimorphic actions are of the social action type, but so are some mimeomorphic actions. Thus the Weberian distinction is not our distinction.

Likewise Weber's *rational action versus traditional action* differs from the polimorphic action versus mimeomorphic action dichotomy. Rational actions come in both polimorphic and mimeomorphic versions, while bureaucracies, the quintessential manifestation of Weber's rational action, contain both kinds of morphicity except in special circumstances.

Of more common distinctions such as *highly valued versus not highly valued, skilled versus unskilled, creative versus dull,* and *meaningful versus mindless,* we have shown throughout the book that these ideas do not correspond to the polimorphic versus mimeomorphic. There is also no match to categories such as *moral versus amoral* or the Foucauldian distinction between *disciplined versus free action.*[8]

The consequence of the diversion of the morphicity distinction from all these other distinctions is seen clearly when we look at the analysis of what is mechanizable and what is not. In principle, all mimeomorphic

---

6. Again, chapter 5 shows that the psychological distinction between internalization versus self-conscious execution of actions is not the same as the polimorphic–mimeomorphic dichotomy for the same reason as was explained in the Dreyfus and Dreyfus case. In the same way, the shape of actions dichotomy cuts across the enculturational versus algorithmic models of learning put forward by Collins because some mimeomorphic actions are learned through enculturation (Collins 1985, 1992).

7. Simon (1969, 1973).

8. Foucault (1977), Kusch (1991).

actions are mechanizable (though some of these may be too complicated to mechanize). Some mimeomorphic actions may be mechanizable with appropriately engineered feedback machines such as neural nets, car washes, and old boots. The way the engineering is done, whether by a digitized realization of a formula or by engineered feedback, is not a crucial dividing line in our theory. For Dreyfus the invention of the neural net promises a significant extension of automation into the realm of what we see as polimorphic actions; for us it does not.[9]

Features of the Morphicity Distinction

The special features of the morphicity dichotomy are most clearly seen in mimeomorphic actions. The idea of mimeomorphic actions creates a meeting ground for actions and mere behaviors, whereas in previous theories these were marked by opposition. Mimeomorphic actions partake of both natural and social kind qualities. The element of coextension allows us to see how the realm of machines interacts with the realm of humans: The two realms can interact where humans intentionally act like machines, shaping their actions by reference to the actions' behavioral instantiations.[10] This is why our theory gives different boundaries to the domain of mechanization as compared to other theories.

Questions and Answers

What can humans do? What can machines do? How do humans delegate actions to machines? How do humans cooperate, and what kind of social organizations are there? How do humans exploit other human cultures? These were the questions with which we began.

Humans can do two kinds of actions and they can merely behave. Machines can merely behave. Where that behavior matches the behavioral instantiation of mimeomorphic actions, machines can behave like humans and be their proxies. Where the behavior does not match the instantiation of mimeomorphic actions, machines are tools, novelties,

9. See Dreyfus (1996), Collins (1996).

10. It might be worth investigating whether autistic persons are a class of humans that can act, but only in a mimeomorphic way.

broken or useless; that is how delegation is done. Humans cooperate in a variety of ways depending on whether their interactions are mediated by mimeomorphic or polimorphic actions; this gives rise to a variety of organizational forms. In social organizations, only those parts of the organization that are mediated by mimeomorphic actions can be replaced by machines.

Mimeomorphic actions should not be confused with ubiquitous skills. Humans can exploit other cultures only by exploiting the mimeomorphic actions or the mere behavior of the exploited. (Or they can colonize and convert the culture.)

Philosophy, Sociology, History

Developing the dichotomy and the answers to the questions has been a matter of philosophical sociology or "sociophilosophy." But this endeavor cannot answer every question. Most actions vary historically in the way they are generally carried out: There are actions, such as love letter writing or marching, in which the morphicity is almost part of the definition of the action, but even in such cases we can imagine exceptions and we can imagine historical periods or other cultures in which even these actions would be different. Golf club swinging, most economically thought of as a mimeomorphic action, has varied according to the coaching fashion and can vary according to the intent (teaching, clowning, and so forth); voting, one of our examples of an occasioned polimorphic action, is usually carried out in the British Parliament as a casual mimeomorphic action because members of parliament simply walk through one voting lobby or another according to party instructions (without worrying about exactly how they place their feet or arms); assembly-line work is mimeomorphic only under a strictly Taylorist regime; before the age of the dial and the automated exchange, reaching the desired party on the telephone involved negotiations with the operator—it had far more elements of polimorphicity than it does nowadays; and the automation of the air pump is still going on. Thus understanding the mixture of polimorphic and mimeomorphic actions within the many actions trees that make up a domain of knowledge is a matter of understanding social history as well as understanding the nature of knowledge.

Likewise, we need to understand social life to know to what extent actors are committed to carrying out an action in one way rather than another, and thus to know what might be changed in order that automation becomes a possibility. To this extent, understanding the potential for automation means, among other things, understanding the extent to which people are ready to begin to execute their actions mimeomorphically; this is a matter of sociology and social history.

References

Achesome, J., and N. J. Amsterdam Norwood. (1629) *The Military Garden, Edinburgh 1629.* Johnson, Inc. and Theatrum Orbis Terrarum [Facsimile edition 1974, edited by J. Walton].

Agre, P. E. (1994) "Surveillance and Capture: Two Models of Privacy." *The Information Society* 10, 2: 101–127.

Akrich, M. (1987) "Comment decrite les objects techniques." *Technique et Culture* 5: 49–63.

Allende, I. (1991) *The Stories of Eva Luna.* London: Penguin.

Amerine, R., and J. Bilmes. (1979) "Following Instruction." Unpublished manuscript, University of California, Santa Barbara.

Anomymous, a. (1982) *How to manage training in units, Field manual no. 25–2.* Washington, D.C.: Department of the Army.

Anonymous, b. (1914) *Recruit Training (Infantry) 1914: An Aid to All Instructors, By Two Officers of the Dorsetshire Regiment.* London: Harrison & Sons.

Anonymous, c. (1992) "Gyrostar." *Japan Pictorial Quarterly Magazine* 15, 2: 24.

Anscombe, G. E. M. (1976) "The Question of Linguistic Idealism." *Acta Philosophica Fennica,* 28: 188–215.

Anscombe, G. E. M. (1979) *Intention,* 2d ed. Oxford: Basil Blackwell.

Barley, S. R., and B. Bechky. (1994) "In the Backrooms of Science: Notes on the Work of Science Technicians." *Work and Occupations* 21: 85–126.

Barnes, B. (1983) "Social Life as Bootstrapped Induction." *Sociology* 17: 524–545.

Barnes, B., D. Bloor, and J. Henry. (1996) *Scientific Knowledge: A Sociological Analysis.* London: Athlone Press.

Barret, R. (1598) *The Theorike and Practike of Moderne Warres, London 1598.* Amsterdam and New York: Da Capo Press and Theatrum Orbis Terrarum Ltd [Facsimile edition 1969].

Benn, G. (1992) *Briefe an Elinor Bueller 1930–1937.* Stuttgart: Klett-Cotta.

Berg, M. (1997) *Rationalizing Medical Work: Decision-Support Techniques and Medical Practices.* Cambridge, Mass.: MIT Press.

Bijker, W., T. Hughes, and T. Pinch. (1987) *The Social Construction of Technological Systems.* Cambridge, Mass.: MIT Press.

Bloor, D. (1995) "Idealism and the Social Character of Meaning." Unpublished paper.

Bloor, D. (1997) *Wittgenstein, Rules, and Institutions.* London: Routledge.

Bratman, M. (1987) *Intentions, Plans, and Practical Reason.* Cambridge, Mass.: Harvard University Press.

Braverman, H. (1974) *Labor and Monopoly Capital: The Degradation of Work in the Twentieth Century.* New York: Monthly Review Press.

Bright, J. R. (1958) *Automation and Management.* Boston: Graduate School of Business Administration, Harvard University.

Burns, T., and G. M. Stalker. (1961) *The Management of Innovation.* London: Tavistock.

Chisholm, R. M. (1970) "The Structure of Intention." *Journal of Philosophy* 67: 633–647.

Clemson, G., and C. G. M. Turregano. (1990) "Emphasis: Simplicity" *Army Trainer,* 10, 1: 30–31.

Collins, H. M. (1974) "The TEA Set: Tacit Knowledge and Scientific Networks." *Science Studies* 4: 165–186.

Collins, H. M. (1975) "The Seven Sexes: A Study in the Sociology of a Phenomenon, or The Replication of Experiments in Physics," *Sociology* 9: 205–224.

Collins, H. M. (1981) "Stages in the Empirical Programme of Relativism," *Social Studies of Science* 11: 3–10.

Collins, H. M. (1983) "The Meaning of Lies: Accounts of Action and Participatory Research," in G. N. Gilbert and P. Abell, eds. *Accounts and Action: Surrey Conferences on Sociological Theory and Method 1.* Aldershot: Gower 69–78.

Collins, H. M. (1985) *Changing Order: Replication and Induction in Scientific Practice.* Beverley Hills: Sage [2nd Edition, Chicago: University of Chicago Press, 1992].

Collins, H. M. (1989) "Computers and the Sociology of Scientific Knowledge." *Social Studies of Science* 19: 613–624.

Collins, H. M. (1990) *Artificial Experts: Social Knowledge and Intelligent Machines.* Cambridge, Mass.: MIT Press.

Collins, H. M. (1992) "Reproducing Historical Experiments: Three Ways of Assembling a Cultural Inventory," paper presented to International Workshop on Reproduction of Historic Experiments, Carl von Ossietzky University of Oldenburg. 24–28 August 1992 (available from the author).

Collins, H. M. (1993) "The Structure of Knowledge." *Social Research* 60: 95–116.

Collins, H. M. (1996) "Embedded or Embodied: Hubert Dreyfus's *What Computers Still Can't Do.*" *Artificial Intelligence* 80, 1: 99–117.

Collins, H. M. (1997) "Rat Tale: Sociology's Contribution to the Problem of Human and Machine Cognition in Context:" In P. J. Feltovich, K. M. Ford, and R. R. Hoffman, eds. *Human and Machine Expertise in Context.* Cambridge, Mass.: AAAI/MIT Press 293–311.

Collins, H. M., and R. Harrison. (1975) "Building a TEA Laser: The Caprices of Communication." *Social Studies of Science* 5: 441–445.

Collins, H. M., and M. Kusch. (1995) "Two Kinds of Actions: A Phenolmenological Study." *Philosophy and Phenomenological Research* 55: 799–819.

Collins, H. M., and M. Kusch. (1995) "Automating Airpumps: An Empirical and Conceptual Analysis." *Technology and Culture* 36: 802–829.

Collins, H. M., and T. J. Pinch. (1982) *Frames of Meaning: The Social Construction of Extraordinary Science.* London: Routledge and Kegan Paul.

Collins, H. M., and T. J. Pinch. (1993) *The Golem: What Everyone Should Know About Science.* Cambridge: Cambridge University Press [Canto paperback edition 1994].

Collins, H. M., and S. Yearley. (1992) "Epistemological Chicken," in A. Pickering ed. *Science as Practice and Culture.* Chicago: University of Chicago Press 301–326.

Collins, H. M., G. de Vries, and W. Bijker. (1997) "Ways of Going On: Skill, Action and Behavioural Repertoires." *Science, Technology and Human Values* 22, 3: 267–284.

Cruso, J. (1632) *Militarie Instructions for the Cavallerie, Cambridge 1632.* Amsterdam and New York: Da Capo Press and Theatrum Orbis Terrarum Ltd [Facsimile edition 1968].

Danto, A. C. (1973) *Analytical Philosophy of Action.* Cambridge: Cambridge University Press.

Davidson, D. (1982) *Essays on Actions and Events.* Oxford: Clarendon Press.

Davidson, D. (1984) *Inquiries into Truth and Interpretation.* Oxford: Clarendon Press.

Davies, E. (1619) *The Art of War and Englands Traynings, London 1619.* Amsterdam and New York: Da Capo Press and Theatrum Orbis Terrarum Ltd [Facsimile edition 1968].

De Landa, M. (1991) *War in the Age of Intelligent Machines.* Cambridge, Mass.: Zone Books.

Dennett, D. C. (1991) *Consciousness Explained.* London: Allen Lane, The Penguin Press.

Dretske, F. (1991) *Explaining Behavior: Reasons in a World of Causes.* Cambridge, Mass.: MIT Press.

Dreyfus, H. L. (1972) *What Computers Can't Do.* New York: Harper & Row.

Dreyfus, H. L. (1992) *What Computers Still Can't Do*. Cambridge, Mass.: MIT Press.

Dreyfus, H. L. (1996) "Response to My Critics." *Artificial Intelligence* 80, 1: 171–191.

Dreyfus, H. L., and S. E. Dreyfus. (1986) *Mind Over Machine: The Power of Human Intuition and Expertise in the Era of the Computer*. New York: Free Press.

Dreyfus, H. L., and S. E. Dreyfus. (1988) "Making a Mind Versus Modeling the Brain: Artificial Intelligence at a Branch Point." *Daedalus* 117: 15–44.

Evans-Pritchard, E. (1937) *Witchcraft, Oracles, and Magic among the Azande*. Oxford: Clarendon Press.

Fairbank, A. (1961) *A Handwriting Manual*. London: Faber & Faber [first edition 1931].

Foucault, M. (1977) *Discipline and Punish: The Birth of the Prison*. New York: Pantheon [translated by Alan Sheridan].

Friedman, G. (1955) *Industrial Society: The Emergence of the Human Problems of Automation*. Toronto: Free Press.

Frith, U. (1989) *Autism: Explaining the Enigma*. Oxford: Blackwell.

Fuss, D. (1989) *Essentially Speaking: Feminism, Nature and Difference*. New York: Routledge.

Garcia Marquez, G. (1988) *Love in the Time of Cholera*. London: Penguin.

Garfinkel, H. (1967) *Studies in Ethnomethodology*. Englewood Cliffs, N.J.: Prentice-Hall.

Garson, B. (1988) *The Electronic Sweatshop: How Computers Are Transforming the Office of the Future into the Factory of the Past*. New York: Simon & Schuster.

Gerth, H. H., and C. W. Mills. (1948) *From Max Weber: Essays in Sociology*. London: Routledge and Kegan Paul.

Gilbreth, F. B., and L. M. Gilbreth. (1914) *Applied Motion Study*. New York: Sturgis and Walton.

Goldman, A. I. (1970) *A Theory of Human Action*. Princeton, N.J.: Princeton University Press.

Gouldner, A. W. (1954) *Patterns of Industrial Bureaucracy*. New York: Free Press.

Harris, R. (1987) *The Language Machine*. Ithaca, N.Y.: Cornell University Press.

Hartland, J. (1993) "The Machinery of Medicine: An Analysis of Algorithmic Approaches to Medical Knowledge and Practice." Ph.D. dissertation. University of Bath.

Haugeland, J. (1985) *Artificial Intelligence: The Very Idea*. Cambridge, Mass.: MIT Press.

Heelan, P. (1983) *Space Perception and the Philosophy of Science.* Berkeley: University of California Press.

Heidegger, M. (1962) *Being and Time.* Oxford: Blackwell [translated by John Macquarrie and Edward Robinson].

Hendriks, R. (1995) "Reductionism, Humanism, and the Care of Autistic Youths." Paper presented to Fourth Bath Quinquennial Science Studies Conference on Humans, Animals, Machines, University of Bath, July 27–31, 1995.

Hobbs, M. (1991) *From the Fairway.* London: The Apple Press.

Janowitz, M. (1960) *The Professional Soldier.* Glencoe, Ill.: The Free Press.

Jenkins, S. P. R. (1994) "Conscious and Unconscious Control in Highly Learned Motor Actions." PhD dissertation. Department of Experimental Psychology, University of Oxford.

Johnson, J. (1988) "Mixing Humans and Nonhumans Together: The Sociology of Door-Closer." *Social Problems* 35: 298–311 [Johnson is a pseudonym of Bruno Latour].

Johnson, M. (1987) *The Body in the Mind: The Bodily Basis of Meaning, Imagination, and Reason.* Chicago: University of Chicago Press.

Jones, B. (1982) "Destruction or Redistribution of Engineering Skills: The Case of Numerical Control." in S. Wood, ed. *The Degradation of Work?* London: Hutchinson 179–200.

Jones, B. (1997) *Forcing the Factory of the Future: Cybernation and Societal Institutions.* Cambridge University Press.

Keegan, J. (1976) *The Face of Battle.* London: Jonathan Cape.

Keegan, J. (1993) *A History of Warfare.* London: Hutchinson.

Keegan, J., R. Holmes, and J. Gau. (1985) *Soldiers: A History of Men in Battle.* London: Hamish Hamilton.

Kellie, T. (1627) *Pallas Armata or Militarie Instructions, Edinburgh 1627.* Amsterdam and New York: Da Capo Press and Theatrum Orbis Terrarum Ltd [Facsimile edition 1971].

Kusch, M. (1989) *Language as Calculus vs Language as the Universal Medium: A Study in Husserl, Heidegger, and Gadamer.* Dordrecht: Kluwer.

Kusch, M. (1991) *Foucault's Strata and Fields: An Investigation into Archaeological and Genealogical Science Studies.* Dordrecht: Kluwer.

Kusch, M. (1995) *Psychologism: A Case Study in the Sociology of Philosophical Knowledge.* London: Routledge.

Kusch, M. (1996) "Sociophilosophy and the Sociology of Philosophical Knowledge," in S. Knuuttila and I. Niiniluoto, eds. *The Methods of Philosophy.* Helsinki: Acta Philosophica Fennica 83–97.

Kusch, M. (1997) "The Sociophilosophy of Folk Psychology," *Studies in the History and Philosophy of Science* 28: 1–25.

Kusch, M. (1998) *Psychological Knowledge: A Social History and Philosophy.* London: Routledge.

Kusterer, K. C. (1978) *Know-How on the Job: The Important Working Knowledge of "Unskilled" Workers.* Boulder: Westview Press.

Lagerspetz, E. (1995) *The Opposite Mirrors: An Essay on the Conventionalist Theory of Institutions.* Dordrecht: Kluwer.

Langley, P., H. A. Simon, G. L. Bradshaw, and J. M. Zytkow. (1987) *Scientific Discovery: Computational Explorations of the Creative Process.* Cambridge, Mass: MIT Press.

Latour, B. (1987) *Science in Action.* Milton Keynes: Open University Press.

Latour, B. (1993) *We Have Never Been Modern.* New York: Harvester Wheatsheaf [transl. by C. Porter].

Latour, B., and S. Woolgar. (1979) *Laboratory Life.* Beverley Hills: Sage.

Lave, J. (1988) *Cognition in Practice.* Cambridge: Cambridge University Press.

Le Carré, J. (1963) *The Spy Who Came in from the Cold.* London: Victor Gollancz Ltd.

Lipscombe, B. (1989) "Expert Systems and Computer-Controlled Decision Making in Medicine." *AI and Society* 3: 184–197.

MacKenzie, D. (1994) "The Automation of Proof: A Historical and Sociological Exploration." University of Edinburgh PICT working paper; no. 56.

MacKenzie, D., and G. Spinardi. (1995) "Tacit Knowledge, Weapons Design, and the Uninvention of Nuclear Weapons." *American Journal of Sociology* 101: 44–99.

Mazlish, B. (1993) *The Fourth Discontinuity: The Co-evolution of Humans And Machines.* New Haven, Conn.: Yale University Press.

McDermott, D. (1981) "Artificial Intelligence Meets Natural Stupidity," in J. Haugeland, ed. *Mind Design.* Cambridge Mass.: MIT Press, 143–160.

Minsky, M. (1987) *The Society of Mind.* London: Heinemann.

Moya, C. J. (1990) *The Philosophy of Action: An Introduction.* Cambridge: Polity Press.

Nadler, G. (1963) *Work Design.* Homewood, Ill.: R. D. Irwin.

Noble, D. F. (1984) *Forces of Production: A Social History of Industrial Automation.* New York: Knopf.

Norman, D. N. (1988) *The Design of Everyday Things.* New York: Doubleday.

Noyes III, H. F. (1991) "Taking the Helplessness Out of Small-Unit Leadership." *Army Trainer* 10, 3: 8–9.

Pearce, C. (1981) *The Little Manual of Calligraphy.* London: Collins.

Pickering, A., ed. (1992) *Science as Practice and Culture.* Chicago, Ill: University of Chicago Press.

Pinch, T., H. M. Collins, and L. Carbone. (1996) "Inside Knowledge: Second Order Measures of Skill." *Sociological Review* 44, 2: 163–186.

Polanyi, M. (1958) *Personal Knowledge.* London: Routledge and Kegan Paul.

Procter, T. (1578) *Of the Knowledge and Conducte of Warres, 1578.* Amsterdam and New York: Da Capo Press and Theatrum Orbis Terrarum Ltd [Facsimile edition 1970].

Rabinbach, A. (1990) *The Human Motor: Energy, Fatigue, and the Origins of Modernity.* New York: Basic Books.

Ramsey, J. L. (1992) "On Refusing to Be an Epstemologically Black Box: Instruments in Chemical Kinetics During the 1920s and '30s." *Studies in the History and Philosophy of Science* 23: 283–304.

Rostand, E. (1942) *Cyrano de Bergerac.* Oxford: Blackwell.

Rubinstein, D. (1977) "The Concept of Action in the Social Sciences." *Journal of the Theory of Social Behaviour* 7: 2–26.

Searle, J. (1980) "Minds, Brains and Programs." *The Behavioural and Brain Sciences* 3: 417–424.

Searle, J. (1983) *Intentionality.* Cambridge: Cambridge University Press.

Searle, J. (1995) *The Construction of Social Reality.* London: Allen Lane.

Shapin, S. (1994) *A Social History of Truth: Civility and Science in Seventeenth-Century England.* Chicago, Ill.: University of Chicago Press.

Shapin, S., and S. Schaffer. (1987) *Leviathan and the Air Pump: Hobbes, Boyle and the Experimental Life.* Princeton: Princeton University Press.

Simon, H. A. (1969) *The Science of the Artificial.* Cambridge, Mass.: MIT Press.

Simon, H. A. (1973) "The Structure of Ill-Structured Problems." *Artificial Intelligence* 4: 181–281.

Smith, B. C. (1988) *Bureaucracy and Political Power.* Brighton: Wheatsheaf.

Stouffer, S. A. (1949) *The American Soldier.* Vol. I. *Adjustment During Army Life.* Princeton, N.J.: Princeton University.

Strum, S., and B. Latour. (1978) "The Meanings of the Social: From Baboons to Humans." *Social Science Information* 26: 783–802.

Suchman, L. (1987) *Plans and Situated Actions: The Problem of Human Machine Communication.* Cambridge: Cambridge University Press.

Suchman, L. (1993) "Response to Vera and Simon's Situated Action: A Symbolic Interpretation." *Cognitive Science* 17: 71–75.

Suen, C. Y. (1983) "Handwriting Generation, Perception and Recognition." *Acta Psychologica* 54: 295–312.

Sundstrom, E., De Meuse, K. P., and Futrell, D. (1990) "Work Teams: Applications and Effectiveness." *American Psychologist* 45: 120–133.

Tuomela, R. (1995) *The Importance of Us: A Philosophical Study of Basic Social Notions.* Stanford, Cal.: Stanford University Press.

Turing, A. M. (1950) "Computing Machinery and Intelligence." *Mind* 59, No. 236: 433–460. Reprinted in D. Hofstadter and D. Dennett, eds. *The Mind's I.* Harmondworth: Penguin (1982), 53–66.

Turner, S. (1994) *The Social Theory of Practices: Tradition, Tacit Knowledge and Presuppositions.* Oxford: Polity Press.

Turregano, C., and M. Walsh (1990) "Fitness Focus: Simplicity." *Army Trainer* (Fall): 30–31.

Vallacher, R. R., and D. M. Wegner. (1985) *A Theory of Action Identification.* Hillsdale, N.J.: Lawrence Erlbaum Associates.

Van Creveld, M. (1989) *Technology and War: From 2000 B.C. to the Present.* New York: The Free Press.

Vermes, G. (1994) "The War Over the Scrolls." *New York Review of Books.* XLI, 14: 10–13.

von Wright, G. H. (1971) *Explanation and Understanding.* London: Routledge and Kegan Paul.

Walton, R. E. (1985) "From Control to Commitment in the Workplace." *Harvard Business Review* 63, 2: 76–84.

Winch, P. G. (1958) *The Idea of a Social Science.* London: Routledge and Kegan Paul.

Winograd, T. (1995) "Heidegger and Computer Systems." In A. Feenberg and A. Hannay, eds. *Technology and the Politics of Knowledge.* Bloomington: Indiana University Press 108–127.

Winograd, T., and Flores, F. (1986) *Understanding Computers and Cognition: A New Foundation for Design.* New Jersey: Ablex.

Wittgenstein, L. (1953) *Philosophical Investigations.* Oxford: Blackwell.

Wray, D. (1987) *Writing.* Leamington Spa: Scholastic Publications.

Index